The Pathwork of Relationship

CREATING
UNION

D0027197

The Pathwork Series:

General Editor: Donovan Thesenga

The Pathwork of Self-Transformation.
Eva Pierrakos.
Bantam, 1990. ISBN 0-553-34896-5.

Fear No Evil; The Pathwork Method of Transforming The Lower Self.
Eva Pierrakos and Donovan Thesenga.
Pathwork Press, 1993. ISBN 0-9614777-2-5.

Creating Union; The Pathwork of Relationship.
Eva Pierrakos and Judith Saly.
Pathwork Press, 1993. ISBN 0-9614777-3-3.

The Undefended Self; Living The Pathwork of Spiritual Wholeness.
Susan Thesenga.
Pathwork Press, 1994. ISBN 0-9614777-4-1.

Publisher: **Pathwork Press**
Route 1, Box 86, Madison, VA 22727 Phone/Fax 703 948-5508
President: Gene Humphrey
Design, Publicity, and Book Orders: Karen Millnick

The Pathwork of Relationship

CREATING
UNION

Compiled and edited by
Judith Saly
from material channeled by
Eva Pierrakos

Pathwork Press
Madison, Virginia
1993

5/97

Library of Congress Catalog Card Number: 93-86256

Psychology: Self-Help
        Relationship

ISBN 0-9614777-3-3

$12.00

Cover Design: Karen Millnick.

Cover Art: Brancusi, Constantin. The Kiss, c. 1912.
        Philadelphia Museum of Art: The Louise and Walter Arensberg
        Collection.

Chapters 3, 4, and 9 appeared in *The Pathwork of Self-Transformation*, Bantam New Age, 1990. Chapter 9 and a portion of Chapter 10 appeared in *Fear No Evil*, Pathwork Press, 1993.

PRINTED IN THE UNITED STATES OF AMERICA

Bookstore

Authorship

Two names appear on the cover of this book: Eva Pierrakos and Judith Saly. Yet neither Eva nor I wrote this book. Eva was the channel through whom "the Guide," a spirit entity of great wisdom, spoke; and who, in the span of twenty-two years, gave us a wealth of material on spiritual transformation. I am the person who was drawn to gather together the Guide's teachings on the subject of relationship, to select, organize, and edit the material, and to present it in the form of a book.

I gratefully acknowledge the editorial comments and suggestions of John Saly, Gene and Peg Humphrey, Susan Thesenga and Jan Bresnick, and the technical assistance of Karen Millnick, Hedda Koehler, and Rebecca Daniels.

This book is the third volume in *The Pathwork Series*, and was commissioned by the Pathwork Foundation. Donovan Thesenga is the editorial director of *The Pathwork Series*.

Judith Saly
New York
October 1993

From the Guide

"These lectures are principally designed for people who follow a path of intensive self-development, such as the Pathwork. The lectures affect areas of the soul which are not accessible unless such a path is taken. Then you will hear an inner echo, *beyond* a mere intellectual and theoretical grasp of the subject.

"Complete understanding may come only later, when the layers of consciousness have opened up. However, all those who work on themselves seriously will eventually be able to make use of the lectures in an entirely different way from those who merely read them without doing the personal work. The difference is distinct.

"When you lack the inner experience of 'Yes, this is true, it affects me on the deepest level of my being,' because you don't practice a vital form of self-development, you may find the lectures to be either merely interesting, self-evident material, or far-fetched theoretical treatises.

"Being affected deep within your being will enable you to further transcend yourself, to understand your problems in a profound way.

"Self-exploration makes new layers of your psyche accessible to your awareness. My words are aimed directly at these layers as they become free to receive the teachings."

Contents

Eva Pierrakos,
the Guide,
and the Pathwork

The material that is gathered here was originally spoken, not written. Eva said that she was not the author of this material, only the channel through which it was delivered. The true author was a discarnate being who spoke through Eva when she entered a state of altered consciousness. This being tells us nothing about itself—no personality traits, no history, no "glamour." It does not even give itself a name, but it came to be known as "the Guide." The material that was transmitted are the "Guide lectures," and the process for personal transformation given in the teachings is known as "the Pathwork."

The Guide placed all emphasis on the material delivered and none on the source. He said, "Do not be concerned with the phenomenon of this communication as such. The only thing important to understand is that there are levels of reality which you have not yet explored and experienced and about which you can only theorize at best.... Do remember that this voice does not express the conscious mind of the human instrument through whom I speak. Furthermore, take into consideration that every human personality has a depth of which he or she may as yet be unaware. At this depth, everybody possesses the means to transcend the narrow confines of his or her own personality and receive access to other realms and to entities endowed with a wider and deeper knowing."

Eva delivered 258 Guide lectures on the nature of psychological and spiritual reality and on the process of personal spiritual development from 1957 to 1979, when she died. She was born in Austria, daughter of the well-known novelist Jakob Wassermann. She came to the United States in 1939. In 1967 she met Dr. John Pierrakos, a psychiatrist and co-creator of a school of therapy known as bio-energetics. A few years later they were married, and the merger of his work and hers led to a great expansion of the Pathwork community. The network of people practicing and teaching the Pathwork now includes four major centers that teach the Pathwork, and study groups in many urban areas in the United States, Europe and South America.

The editor of this book, Judith Saly, has also edited *The Pathwork of Self-Transformation* (Bantam, 1990) and is the author of *How To Have A Better Relationship* (Blue Cliff Editions, Ballantine, 1987). She has studied and practiced the Pathwork teachings since 1958 and has been a Pathwork teacher for twenty-five years. She was part of the group which founded the Phoenicia Pathwork Center, and has also served as president of the Pathwork Foundation. Judith married John Saly in 1995. They have three children and two grandchildren and alternately reside in New York City and Phoenicia.

Introduction

If life is a school, relationship is its university. It is through your relationships, especially through your relationship with your love-partner that you can learn and grow most. We are born woman and man, and we long for each other for we need each other, we need to become united with the "other" physically, emotionally, and spiritually. This longing is built into our genetic codes, and finding one's life partner is at the very center of human life.

But how many times do you see a couple whose relationship, after years of being together, is still vibrantly alive, where you sense harmony and delight, communication which is deep and lighthearted at the same time, where you know that both partners have accepted their mate totally, in surrender to the divine force of love, where differences are considered challenges to understand each other more deeply, trusting that all problems can be worked out? Hardly ever.

From looking at the statistics, one would conclude that to live with another person is for many an unbearable burden and not the harmonious state people expect when they marry. And even when two people stay together and continue to love each other, there are moments when they feel frustrated, when they bicker, when they feel estranged from each other. Is it possible to overcome the difficulties, to heal the wounds?

The approach of this book is very different from others on relationship. *The Guide sets the woman-man conflict against the vast context of cosmic forces,* illuminating it from the high perspective of one who is beyond the duality of the two sexes.

From that vantage point he also sees into our hearts and souls, where we ourselves are divided. He maps out a road toward self-unification and, through that, toward blissful union with another human being. His teachings are truly unique in their scope as well as in their practicality.

The history of anyone's relationships reveals the inner landscape of that person's being. From such a history one can deduce the person's beliefs about life, the opposite sex, love and sexuality in general, about marriage, and so on. If you learn to look at yourself with a somewhat detached, but nevertheless passionately curious interest, and with honesty, you will be surprised at what you discover: it was you who co-created the present status of your relationship, or the lack of it. It did not just happen to you. You are not a victim.

One likes to believe that any trouble in one's relationship is caused by outside circumstances, or the other partner. If only he, or she, would change, how perfect life would be! Well, this is the greatest fallacy. Even if we assumed that you are an angel and your husband, wife, or companion is a fiend, aren't you responsible for choosing and staying with such a partner? But we are not assuming that you are an angel. We—you and I— know that you do have an angelic light inside of you, which we can call the higher self: a loving, caring, selfless, creative core. But we also know that there is a less attractive layer around that divine core: the selfish, vindictive, distrustful lower self, which is responsible for the many pains we suffer and inflict on others, especially on those closest to us. Without getting acquainted with this layer, without finding out how it came into existence, without owning up to it, we cannot transform it. No matter how hard we try to pretend that this ugly layer doesn't exist, no matter how much we attempt to hide it, disown it, or meditate it away, it will not dissolve unless we face it directly and begin to transform it consciously.

Mostly, we are not even aware of the existence of this lower self. The Guide is teaching us to become alert to it. It is not enough to dig into one's childhood history and connect the present relationship with one's early experiences with father or mother, though those are very significant and will furnish many clues. Yet in the landscape of our souls the lower self and its effects also need to be discovered. Without facing what we like least about ourselves, we cannot understand why we don't have a well-working relationship, let alone make a significant change.

Many problems in the area of relationship are caused by feelings and thoughts that are buried in the *unconscious*. Such unexamined thoughts and feelings have their own erroneous childish logic. They cause conflicts in the soul. And if there is a war within your own soul, how can you have a healthy relationship with someone else? The contradictory, unresolved feelings and thoughts within the self need to be brought to light first. But how do you recognize the inner conflicts and how can you work toward resolving them?

The answers are in your inner, divine core.

What are your *unconscious* beliefs about men, or women? What are your *unconscious* feelings about loving, about marriage? With proper guidance, it is possible to find out. When the unconscious becomes conscious, you may discover thoughts like these:

"If I love, I will be hurt."

"If I show my feelings, I will be rejected."

"Marriage is slavery."

"I am not supposed to be happy."

These, and similar "images," as the Guide calls them, need to come to the surface. "You will not know what your personal buried convictions are until you discover them with a sudden feeling of relief. For unconscious, or half-conscious feelings are self-fulfilling prophecies: According to your belief it shall be given to you." Who knows what lurks in your unconscious? If your past relationships followed definite patterns, often unproductive or even destructive, set yourself the goal of finding out why they came into existence, and how you can stop your compulsion to recreate them.

To be able to examine what you, deep down, really believe about the possibility of finding your life-partner, or about improving the relationship you have, you need to learn much about yourself, on all levels of your being.

The Guide gives us very practical instructions on how to discover ourselves and how to do the work of self-transformation —with, or without the cooperation of our partner, with, or without being in a relationship. He teaches us *how to get from where we are to where we want to be.* His are not superficial exercises, but methods that imply a willingness to open one's eyes, to face oneself in truth without sentimentality, to walk on a spiritual path. Such commitment brings immense rewards: psychological and spiritual growth, authenticity, joy. From these follows the capacity to establish a relationship with a partner equally prepared to relate, reveal, and reciprocate.

You may have already tried to put the other first, give unconditional love, be patient, never threaten, always stay calm and kind. Such noble resolutions can't work for long when they are superimposed on layers and layers of unresolved conflicts not only with your partner but also within your own soul. There is no way around it: *you cannot transcend before you transform.*

This is why, if you want to make changes in your married life, or want to find the right person, or genuinely improve your relationship, you need to find the *roots* of your problems. When you know and accept yourself as you are now, including your lower self, you build on a solid foundation.

The Guide will not give you superficial advice, will not tell you to smile at your partner when you are seething with rage; neither will he tell you to vent that rage in a hurtful and destructive way. He will teach you, though, how to allow yourself to feel all your feelings without unloading them where they don't belong. He will give you astonishing insights into the nature of the female and male forces in the universe, the spiritual meaning of this particular aspect of our dualistic existence: relationship. You can safely take the journey into the jungle of your inner land, because you will be led through the brambles and thickets to the Godself that exists within you and from which all the answers that are personally yours will come in a most natural and simple way. You will come to know that it is in your power to create a positive relationship that works well and brings bliss.

As you read the lectures, open up not only your mind, but become receptive in your whole self. Imagine yourself in the presence of a being of greater love and deeper wisdom than you have ever encountered before. The blessings given at the beginning and end of each lecture carry divine energy. Let them penetrate your soul.

J.S.

PART I

Cosmic Principles and Psychological Concepts

"And the two shall be one"—the words often heard at a marriage ceremony—refer to much more than two people beginning a life together. It is a cosmic statement. "Two"—duality—is the basic condition of our existence on earth, and "One" is the state of unity from which we have separated ourselves and to which we long to return.

Since the state of duality is a split from oneness—from Paradise—it contains pain. We long to return to our lost state of bliss. Transforming that in ourselves which is the cause of our separateness, of our inability to relate well and to allow the unhindered flow of love, is the goal of the pathwork of relationship.

Every spiritual path shows a way from self-alienation to self-finding and therefore God-finding. The teachings in this book follow ancient esoteric traditions, yet they are contemporary in their exquisite comprehension of human psychology. Unity contains all, and therefore also the divine principles underlying our earthly duality: the masculine and feminine energies whose flesh-and-blood manifestations we, men and women, are. The channeled material in the first part of the book describes these cosmic principles and explains how they relate to the spiritual meaning and psychology of the man-woman relationship.

Seen from this greater perspective, the struggles we all make to find a love partner, to keep that love alive, to continually deepen that love, takes on a new depth and dignity. For in this endeavor we are not only doing the work of overcoming our fears of giving up our separateness in order to claim for ourselves a richer and happier life, but we are also co-creators in a great cosmic movement, that of the further evolution of the universe. Our yearning for a deeper union in love with another is so compellingly powerful because of its cosmic significance. Here we see the link between our individual, temporal lives and the greater reality that encompasses us.

Understanding the functioning of the masculine and feminine principles in the universe will vastly enrich your comprehension of the significance of your personal yearning for a deeper union in love with another. Embark on this flight of imagination into a new space, be a cosmic traveler, and return with new insights and new hope.

J.S.

Relationship

Greetings, my dearest friends. I welcome you and I bless you.
"What is life?" is a question asked by many. *Life is relation-ship, my friends.* Other answers can be given, and they all may be truthful. But above all else, life is relationship. If you do not relate at all, you do not live. Your life, or your relationships, are relative to your attitude. You may relate positively or negatively. But the moment you relate, you live. That is why *the person who relates negatively is more alive than the person who relates little.* Destructive relationships lead to a climax that is ultimate-ly bound to dissolve the destructiveness. But non-relating, usu-ally under the guise of false serenity, is further down the scale.

Every affliction of the psyche prevents relating to others. Fruitful relating can exist only to the degree the soul is healthy and free. But first one has to understand more profoundly what relating is.

The Plan of Evolution

Remember that *the whole plan of evolution is about uniting, bringing together individual consciousnesses,* for only in this way can separateness be given up. Union with an abstract idea, with an intangible God, or as a cerebral process, is not really union. Only the actual contact of one individual with another establishes those conditions in the entire personality that are the pre-requisites for true inner union and unity. Therefore this pull manifests as a tremendous force, moving people toward each other, making separateness painful and empty. The life force is therefore permeated not only with the pull toward others, but also with pleasure supreme. *Life and pleasure are one.* Life, pleasure, contact with others, oneness with others, are the goal of the cosmic plan.

Relationships With All Things and Beings

You are used to associating the word "relationship" only with human beings. But in truth, this word applies to everything, even to inanimate objects, to concepts and ideas. It applies to the circumstances of living, to the world, to yourself, to your thoughts and attitudes. To the degree you relate, you will not feel frustrated but will have a sense of fulfillment.

The scale of the possibilities of relationship is very wide. Let us begin with the lowest form on earth, which is mineral. Since a mineral is without consciousness, you may believe that it does not relate. That is untrue. Since it lives, it does relate, but its degree of relating is limited to its degree of life or, more correctly put, it is a mineral *because* it is incapable of relating more. The mineral relates by letting itself be perceived and used. Thus it relates in a completely passive way. The relating capacity of an animal is much more dynamic. It actively responds to other animals, to nature, and to human beings.

The Ability to Relate Depends on the Level of Consciousness

The scale of the capacity to relate is much wider among human beings than you even remotely realize. Let us begin with those on the lowest scale among human beings. That would be the completely insane person who has to be put into solitary confinement, or the criminal who is not so different from the former. They are both completely withdrawn, live in outer and inner isolation. They can hardly relate to other human beings. But since they are alive, they must continue to relate somehow. They therefore relate to other aspects of life: to things, to their environment, even if it is in the most negative way, to food, to certain bodily functions, perhaps even to some ideas, or art, or nature. It should be very useful, my friends, to think about life and people from this point of view. Meditating on this subject will help you greatly and will increase your understanding about many things, not the least about your own life.

Now, by contrast, let me immediately go to the highest form of human beings. These are people who relate beautifully; who are deeply involved with others; who are unafraid of involvement; who have no protective covering against experience and feeling. Therefore they love. They permit themselves to love. *In the last analysis, the ability to love always comes down to the inner willingness and readiness to do so.* People belonging in this category love not only abstractly and generally, but they love personally and concretely, regardless of risk. Such people are not necessarily saints, or holy, or anywhere near perfect. They may have their faults. They may be wrong at times and may have negative feelings. But, on the whole, they love, relate, and do not fear involvement. They have freed themselves from their defenses. Such people, in spite of occasional disappointments or setbacks, have a life full of fruitful, meaningful relationships.

What is life for the average person? It is a combination of manifold possibilities. A person may be relatively free and relate well in certain areas of his or her life and be very much obstructed in others. Only deep personal insight will enable you to find the truth in this respect about yourself. When a relationship appears good on the surface, but is devoid of depth and inner meaning, then it is so easy to deceive oneself and say, "Look how many good friends I have! There is nothing wrong with my relationships, and yet I am unhappy, lonely, and unfulfilled." If this is how it is with you, it cannot be true that your relationships are good, or that you are truly willing to relate. You cannot be lonely and unhappy if your relationships are genuine.

On the other hand, if the way in which you relate fulfills a superficial function only, then it may be pleasant and distracting, but somehow shallow. Your true self is never revealed, and therefore you are unfulfilled. Thus you also prevent others from relating and do not give what they search for, whether or not they know it. This is due to your unconscious fear of exposure, letting your friends know about your various inner conflicts. As long as you are not willing to resolve them, you cannot have meaningful relationships—and therefore you must be unfulfilled.

The average person has some capacity and willingness for involvement and relationship, but not enough. The drama of mutual exchange and communication takes place on a superficial level. Unconscious currents affect the involved parties and, if the shallow relationship is a close one, sooner or later it will cause a disturbance. If the shallow relationship never becomes close, nothing will happen, but neither can one deceive oneself that it is a real tie. Unconscious destructive tendencies can only be dissolved if one faces and understands them. This will not harm the relationship, because then the communication will automatically take place on a more profound level and there will be mutual exchange.

It is often not clear to you what constitutes a profound and meaningful relationship: Is the criterion the mutual exchange of ideas or is it the mutual exchange of sexual pleasure? Both may indeed be there, yet their presence will not necessarily make the communication very deep. The only true criterion is how genuine you are, how open and undefended; how willing you are to feel, to involve and expose yourself and all that really matters to you. How many people do you know to whom you can express your real sorrows, needs, worries, longings, wishes? Very few, if any. To the degree you permit yourself to become aware of these feelings you will find more friends with whom you can share and whose life you are capable of truly understanding.

If you shy away from yourself, how can you be willing to communicate to others that which you do not dare to acknowledge to yourself? Thus you must live in isolation and unfulfillment. This is why we are so very much concerned in our work of self-transformation that you learn to admit the truth to yourself. Only then can you begin to have real relationships instead of false ones and lead a full life. Even your relationships to other aspects of life, such as art, nature, ideas, will take on new forms that are very much alive, whereas before you may have used them to avoid troublesome feelings.

Real relating and communication can be confused with the childish compulsion to tell everyone everything. You may share your feelings indiscriminately and jeopardize yourself, in the misunderstanding that foolish candor, or unwise exposure, or cruel "honesty" are proof of your openness and willingness to relate. In reality this merely covers up your withdrawal on a much more hidden level and in a more subtle manifestation. Thus you can produce the "proof" that it does not pay to involve yourself.

With true self-understanding, and the consequent liberation from your self-constructed prison, there will be nothing strained in your self-revelation and your relationships. You will intuitively choose the right people and the right opportunities and the right manner. Occasional misjudgments will never crush you or put you back into hiding. But the organic growing process, the freedom, comes only gradually, and only after you have started to pursue a path of self-knowledge.

Psychiatrists often diagnose people according to their ability to relate and the depth and meaningfulness of their relationships. It has been found that some of the more severely disturbed people can receive help more easily than others whose disturbance is less obvious, because the latter can deceive themselves and pretend that things are not so bad and can continue to hide from the truth within. This subterfuge is not available to those who are more disturbed. They therefore come to a point where they have to make a choice: to look at their inner life squarely, without self-deception, or not. They may also have a severe breakdown which will postpone self-confrontation. But they are nearer the point of decision—which they may reach only in the following life—than the less neurotic person who continues to evade self-confrontation.

Many of you, my friends, do not have a clear concept of what it is to really relate or love. Your concern is mainly centered around yourself. If you are outgoing to others, it is not a natural, spontaneous process, but artificial and compulsive. But the natural concern and warmth for others will come if you persevere on this road. As long as you cannot admit that you are human and that you need help in exposing your vulnerabilities, you cannot form real relationships. Thus your life will remain empty, at least in some important areas.

And now to your questions.

QUESTION: Is it a manifestation of healthy relating if a relationship changes and if a person wishes many relationships? What about seeking variety and flow?

ANSWER: This is again one of those questions that cannot be answered with a "yes" or "no." Both a changing relationship and the desire for variety may indicate healthy or unhealthy motives. Often it is a combination. One must beware of oversimplification. The fact that a relationship changes for the worse does not necessarily indicate relapse or stagnation. It may be a necessary, temporary reaction to an unhealthy submissiveness, to the craving for affection, or to any other one-sided neurotic bondage. Before a healthy relationship can come into being between two people who have been tied together by a variety of mutual distortions, such a temporary outer or inner storm may fulfill the same balancing function that an electric storm or earthquake fulfills in nature.

Whether or not a relationship can become predominantly free and healthy depends on both parties. A smooth outer relationship, apparently devoid of friction, is not necessarily an indication of its intrinsic health and meaningfulness. Close examination of the ties and their significance is the only answer. One can never generalize. When two people grow together in any kind of relationship—be it partnership, love, friendship—they have to go through various phases. If they muster sufficient insight about themselves, and not only about the other, such relationship will become more securely rooted and ever more fruitful.

Seeking a Variety of Relationships

As to seeking variety, that too depends on the real motivation. If variety is sought hastily, compulsively, due predominantly to fear, greed, and grasping, due to being unable to genuinely relate to any one person, and therefore supplementing this lack with a lot of superficial ties, if others are constantly sought as safeguards against being dependent on or deserted by those few with whom a deeper relationship exists, then, needless to say, it indicates unhealthy trends. But if variety is sought in a free spirit because of the richness of different human beings and not in order to use one relationship against the other, then it is healthy. Often, both motivations exist. But even in the former case, there may be a temporary necessity for variety as a reaction to a previous state of withdrawal. Then the seeking of variety may be a step toward health. A negative manifestation is often an indication of a positive transitory phase.

Manipulation

QUESTION: Between two human beings who want to relate, but use a lot of manipulation, where does the element of real love come in? Does the love dissolve the manipulation?

ANSWER: To the degree a person feels the need for manipulation, which is an unconscious protective measure, real love cannot exist. The two elements are mutually exclusive. The pseudo-need for manipulation, if you examine it, stems from egocentric fear and an overcautiousness about letting go to feeling and to being. Manipulation prohibits love, even though some measure of real love may also exist.

If the love is greater than the distortion, it will outweigh the distortion, and thus the relationship will be less problematic. Dissolution of problematic areas can only happen through understanding. Then love can blossom. But where darkness, confusion, and a refusal to face reality exist, love cannot come into being. The fact that you do love does not simply dissolve all the negative currents and distortions, conflicts and fears, unconscious defensive measures and manipulations. It is not as easy as all that.

Your ability to relate is actually simple to measure: your outer life furnishes you with many clues if you but understand them. If a relationship is problematic, unconscious distortions exist in both parties. One alternately blames the other, or wallows in self-blame. It takes some time and understanding to recognize that one wrong does not eliminate another; that all involved are responsible for all the problems of a relationship. Such insight always has a very liberating effect, simply because it is true. Truth will free you of guilt and of the necessity to accuse, blame, and judge.

QUESTION: Isn't it sometimes much easier to relate to somebody one is not too close to? One is less critical.

ANSWER: Why, of course. This is just the proof that it is not a real relationship, but a superficial one. A real relationship means involvement, and that does not mean just looking at the negative aspects and currents. Involvement means the staking of one's whole being. A relationship of deep involvement is bound to suffer friction because there are so many unrecognized and unresolved problem areas within both parties. That is why each friction can become a stepping stone if approached with a constructive attitude. I do not mean that you should have only such deep relationships. That would be impossible and unrealistic. But there must be quite a few, all different, if you are to feel that your life is dynamic and fruitful.

The Harm of Unconscious Expectations
    To be more specific, I may add that unconscious expectations, claims, and demands cause havoc in relationships. This is not because all expectations are necessarily "wrong," but because they smolder underground and cause a mutual strain

as they clash with the demands of the other person. Apart from the fact that some demands are really unjustified and unreasonable—and they can be recognized as such only if they come to your surface awareness—even justified expectations will cause problems if you are unaware of them.

I close with very special blessings for everyone who hears or reads these words, for everyone who enters this work now, who is in it already, or will enter it in the future. I leave you with my love and warmth, and with the promise of active help that can come to you to the degree that you recognize your resistance to self-awareness. Find your willingness to recognize your rationalizations that keep you from truth and reality within yourself, that keep you from growing into a meaningful life. And may you come to know that life is benign. The flow of living is continuous and only in your limited view is there any need to fear. The more you remove the shackles of your self-created blindness, the more will you experience the truth of these words. Be blessed, be in God!

CHAPTER 2

The Masculine and Feminine Principles in the Creative Process

Greetings, my friends. Blessings and love are extended to you and reach you in your deepest being to the extent you open up to them. Receive and let them come into you.

I would like to talk tonight about specific elements of the *creative, universal power.* Every human being possesses and expresses this power. Coming into your own means deliberately, consciously, and purposefully using the creative power *which you are* in your innermost being and which emanates from you. You constantly create your life circumstances with this power, but you do so unconsciously and unknowingly. What you think and feel, what you believe and conceive of, what you secretly wish and fear, shape and determine creative substance and constitute the motor force of this power.

What a tremendous difference it makes when you deliberately, consciously create your fate, rather than unknowingly! Unconsciously creating, you ascribe certain experiences to some obscure fate. Your experiences seem to have little or nothing to do with who you are, what you feel, what you wish, what you believe in right now, or with what you choose to do with your thoughts and feelings. But self-realized individuals know exactly how they create their lives.

It is a great moment when one suddenly understands that it was not hostile fate but one's own doing that brought obstructions and unhappiness about, and sees the secret attitude that produced the unwelcome fate. Once cause and effect are seen to connect, one's fate is no longer subject to a blind and malevolent outer power. From that moment on, the individual ceases to be helpless. In truth, human beings have never been helpless against any force or power outside themselves, but they are helpless against their own inner processes until they recognize and change them.

This is the way of the path. As you discover the root of your negative experience within yourself, you become capable of transforming that experience. To create a positive fate deliberately, it is essential for you to understand more about the creative force of the universe and how you can personally use it.

The Working of the Two Fundamental Principles

There are two fundamental principles through which the creative process works: the first is *activation;* the other is the principle of getting out of the way and *letting it happen.* These two creative principles exist throughout the entire universe and manifest in everything in your life. They regulate all that happens, desirable or undesirable, important or unimportant, from the smallest, most mundane occurrence up to the creation of a universe. If what is created is to be constructive, fruitful, joyful, and pleasurable, these principles must interact in a harmonious way: they must complement one another. If what is created is destructive, painful, wasteful, or unhappy, these two principles must also have been at work, only in this case they have been distorted and misunderstood. Instead of complementing one another, they interfere with one another. Instead of the two aspects making one unitive whole, a dualism makes two mutually exclusive opposites or negations out of them. When both sides of the duality are reconciled, two apparently opposing forces work together toward one goal. Duality versus unity pertains to all of creation: wherever an entity is removed from its center and is therefore in ignorance and error, duality comes into existence. The entire earth sphere, namely human consciousness, is in the dualistic state, so that all perceivable creative functions are split down the middle. The creative process is also affected by the dualistic state of the human consciousness.

The two fundamental principles of creation, activating and letting be, are universal laws present in everything that has ever been created. They are not mechanical laws such as the law of gravity. All laws, even impersonal, physical ones have come into existence from, through, and by consciousness, and must have been created by the combination of these two fundamental principles. Direct creation, with its own specific laws, is always an expression of consciousness, for everything in creation can only be a result of consciousness. Whether the consciousness stems from an individual brain or personality, or whether the consciousness is the great universal spirit permeating all life, does not matter. The principle is the same. Your conscious attitude expresses whether or not you activate or whether or not you let be. These two principles and their roles deserve close scrutiny.

The Masculine Principle

To activate means that the conscious entity deliberately claims, sets in motion, moves toward, causes, determines, or purposefully uses these forces by calling them into action and removing every possible obstruction. Effort and endeavor are an integral part of setting the creative forces in motion. This is active doing. We may call it the masculine principle in creation.

The attitude of "letting be" means to be receptive and to wait. It is also a movement, for anything that is alive must be moving. But this kind of movement is very different from the movement of the activating principle. The activating principle moves out toward another state. The spirit of letting be is a movement within itself; it is a pulsating, involuntary movement, while the movement of activation is deliberate and self-determining. Words are insufficient to explain these facts and you will have to listen with your inner ear and use your imagination and your innermost faculties to perceive what I am telling you here.

The Feminine Principle

The consciousness behind the attitude of letting be is one of patient, trustful waiting, of allowing a ripening process come to fruition, of surrendering to a force set in motion; this may be called the feminine principle in creation. As I have said before, the masculine and feminine principles exist in every endeavor and creative act. The self-determining, voluntary act expresses self-confidence and knowledge of one's divine nature. The going with the creative forces, the surrender to them, expresses deep trust in life and in the state of being that does not require one iota more movement than to activate the very powers one trusts in. Everything that functions well in the universe down to the smallest manifestations of mundane life combines these two aspects of life and consciousness. Nothing can be created without both of these principles being at work. *No union between the sexes can be fulfilling unless these principles function as they are meant to.* Pleasure supreme is possible to the degree these attitudes are healthy, and to the extent that trust in self and life allow both aspects to manifest.

Both men and women represent both principles; only their arrangement, emphasis, degree, proportion, and relation to each other are different. The healthy, integrated man does not represent exclusively the activating principle, nor does the healthy, integrated woman represent exclusively the principle of letting be. Men and women must express both aspects, but the emphasis differs and the areas in which both creative principles manifest or apply also differ.

Once you begin to think about this and look at life with the slightly altered vision that acknowledges both principles at work, you will see and understand a lot more about creation itself as well as about world events. Whether you create a business, a situation between yourself and another person, your own fate, or a universe, all depends to what extent you understand and harmoniously use the masculine and feminine principles of creation and to what degree you are conscious of both principles and allow them both to unfold out of yourself. When these creative principles are distorted and used in erroneous ways they create confusion and disharmony. The result is destruction.

Distortions of the Masculine and Feminine Creative Forces

A man cannot dare to be fully a man and activate the creative force in a deliberate and purposeful way when his unconscious is still steeped in hostility, rage, and anger, because the activating principle then threatens to express these destructive impulses. There are many men as well as women in this world who are still so undeveloped that they have no compunction about expressing their destructive impulses. They do not mind activating the masculine principle, even though it brings forth the most violent and negative actions. Only when development proceeds further and the individual no longer wishes to express violence and destruction will he or she become frightened of his or her own active principle and therefore hold it back. This is why you cannot fully be a man or a woman unless you first come to terms with your negative emotions and desires. When you fully face these feelings, they will lose their power. But as long as you are unaware of their existence, they will control you and force you to act upon them without even knowing what you are doing and why. You will then rationalize them or turn the destructiveness upon yourself, in fear of letting the active principle out and sow its negative seeds.

Thus, in a transitory state of evolution, people prevent themselves from using the activating principle, because all activation would be based on negativity. This explains why so many people find themselves paralyzed in inactivity and stagnation. Temporarily, people will hold themselves back to prevent their misuse of the creative principle. Therefore, healthy activation, self-assertion, and autonomy are also temporarily bound and must wait for release until the personality has settled the difficulty with its own destructive nature. People may have to go through a number of appearances on this earth plane in which their activating forces must be dimmed so as to no longer express the distorted form of the creative principle of activation.

You all need to make contact with your hidden cruelty, brutality, sadism, vindictiveness, and malice, to learn how to truly outgrow these destructive emotions by seeing, understanding and accepting them. Only then do you become genuinely convinced that there is no need for destructiveness. As long as destructiveness is not squarely faced, this conviction is lacking, and you hold back mostly because you are afraid of retribution and other consequences. Only when you have the courage and honesty to fully see and accept the damaging emotions and desires within yourself, only when you totally comprehend and evaluate them, will you see without a shadow of a doubt that they are superfluous as defenses, nor do they serve any other purpose. As these feelings become obsolete and you need no longer be on guard against your own spontaneous reactions, you will be free enough to activate the greatest power in the universe within yourself. You will no longer fear this power, for it will be free from pollution, perversion, and distortion. You can then claim your birthright. You can then call into being your own creative forces.

It often happens that a person is sufficiently cleansed of destructive distortions so as to safely use his or her inner powers, but the old habit-pattern of holding back is so firmly rooted that the personality will needlessly forgo the use of the activating principle, not yet aware that it is safe to use this power. The destructiveness that still exists is no longer dangerous because it is now sufficiently conscious. The person is too alert to allow the destructiveness to rule and precipitate negative actions. The individual does not know yet, however, that with the same power that can handle the remaining aggressions, he or she can also use the greatest forces in the universe that are within the self. Now, becoming godlike, one can use the activating power to create circumstances according to one's own choice.

So we must differentiate between those who rightfully dim their creative activity because they are justifiably afraid of the negative components in it, and those who dim this power simply because they do not know of its positive potential. They are like a person who has been asleep for a very long time and, waking up, has yet to discover the power of all his faculties and the scope of their unfoldment.

The masculine principle is outgoing and leads to action which has consequences. The action following the driving force or impetus actively builds, affects, causes, and determines. When the personality is fully aware of no longer needing and therefore no longer fearing the destructive forces, it also begins to know that it can create. At this point people discover the powers within them and that their minds can activate them.

The feminine principle of receptivity, of letting the activating forces work their lawful way toward fruition, is distorted when the entity refuses self-responsibility. If self-activation is relinquished and, instead of surrendering to the self-activated inner powers, one surrenders to another person's authority, then the role of the creative feminine principle is perverted. By the same token, a woman who surrenders her autonomy to a mate because she is too fearful and lazy to assume the consequences for her own actions makes a travesty and caricature out of femininity. Her surrender will never be motivated by love and trust in him; her aim will not be to experience ecstasy by uniting the two creative principles in this particular manifestation. Instead, she surrenders to him out of fear of life, refusing to assume her obligations in life. Such distorted surrender cannot bring anything favorable to either partner. When a woman wants to be a parasite and burden her partner with the brunt of her responsibilities, she is cheating life, but life cannot be cheated. The result is that she must increase her fear of life, as well as her fear of the man who is supposed to be her authority. She must fear her self-determined enslavement. Thus the feminine principle or femininity is often wrongly associated with helplessness, passivity, and inferiority, while the masculine principle or masculinity is often wrongly associated with brute force and superiority.

In reality, a woman cannot truly be a woman unless she is self-determining. In the terms of this lecture, a woman has to be secure in her selfhood by activating the creative principle within herself, for only when she is accountable for her mistakes and willing to accept and learn from them can she be strong and self-responsible. Then she will be unafraid of total surrender, of letting go, of allowing the involuntary forces in herself to guide her.

Conversely, a man cannot be truly a man when he is not free from destructiveness, and when he is not willing to let the activating principle go to work in its own fashion. In other words, he must observe the feminine principle in order to fully activate the masculine one, just as the full woman must activate the masculine principle in order to give herself over to the feminine.

Harmonious Interaction

This interaction between man and woman expresses the two sides of the creative power in a very obvious way. Union between the sexes is satisfactory to the degree that the two sides are in harmony *within* each partner. Only when that condition is fulfilled can harmony be established *between* them.

As man is justified in fearing the activating forces as long as he is unaware of his destructiveness and therefore cannot control it, so is woman justified in fearing self-surrender as long as she makes herself helpless for whatever distorted motives. If she is not in possession of her inherent powers, surrender must be debilitating and dangerous. Since men and women express both the masculine and feminine principle, they must both cleanse their activating powers of violence and hostility. Both need to learn to ascribe the cause of all that happens to them to the self, rather than blaming outside factors for their suffering.

When working on themselves on a path of self-transformation, both men and women come across the identical lower-self patterns. They find their false aggression, hostility, violence, over-activity, impatience, and refusal to wait for the powers to lawfully come to fruition. They also find their false receptivity and false letting go, that is, denial of self-responsibility, laziness, following the line of least resistance. Trying to find an authority who will take on what is really their responsibility is one such way to evade accountability. Both men and women therefore have to work out the same problems, but their interaction is on a complementary rather than on an identical level.

No self-realization is possible unless you become full men and women in the deepest possible sense. This is why human problems are always primarily concerned with the relationship between the sexes. No matter what other problems you human beings have, they are at least indirectly connected with your masculinity or your femininity. The expression and handling of the masculine and feminine creative principles permeates your whole personality.

The Role of the Two Principles in Any Endeavor

Let us take for example a problem at work. How can your work be successful if the activating principle is lacking or dimmed and if you are not sufficiently outgoing and healthily aggressive, or if you do not activate your own creative powers, but hold them back? What if you let them out, but the activating forces remain hostile and antisocial? In that case you will inevitably get into difficulties with your environment, no matter how accomplished you may be in your profession. If the spirit of love is lacking, you will not want to contribute to life with and through your work. Therefore there can be nothing creative about it and the deeper spiritual powers cannot manifest. If, however, you want to enrich life, you can safely enrich yourself by and through your activity, without falsely feeling guilty about your *healthy* aggression. The creative activation will do justice to both—enriching others and the self in every possible way.

And how can what is activated come to fruition if the feminine creative principle is not allowed to function by letting be, by waiting for fruition, by trusting the forces set in motion? Your own intuitive powers reach your consciousness only when the receptive spirit of letting be reigns after the activation. Then you can be guided according to the highest wisdom, that of creative inspiration, necessary for all successful work. It, too, consists of the two aspects: inspiration must be deliberately activated by the mind, and allowed to flow, take its course, and manifest in its own fashion without interference from the mind.

The laws indicated here are applicable to all endeavors. Whether you do menial labor, or work as an artist, a scientist, or do anything else, the law is the same, although the degree to which these principles must function may vary. Simple menial work can be done mechanically and yet relatively efficiently, though it can also be a creative act when it is done in this spirit. But artistic, scientific, or spiritual work can never succeed unless it follows these laws of creation.

So your work must fail, as your human relationships and partnerships must fail, when the masculine and feminine principles do not properly interact and complement one another. Needless to say that in all these areas the relationship between the two aspects of creation varies in emphasis at any given time or phase.

If one of the two principles functions in a healthy way, the other must also be right. It is impossible for one to be healthy and for the other to be distorted. Hence, the man who has a problem in self-activation in some area of his life must elsewhere be unable to let go and be carried. It would be false to assume that the man who is not sufficiently active and aggressive is so throughout his total personality. He will inevitably discover an area in which he is overactive, over-masculine—precisely where the feminine principle should reign. The distortion is a compensation for the underactivity in the place where he should exert his masculine activating force but does not. Conversely, the man who expresses an exaggerated form of the masculine principle must harbor areas in which he is too passive and expresses the distorted feminine principle. These examples are equally applicable to women.

Balancing the Two Principles Within Each Individual

The manifestation of the masculine and feminine principles in the inner life of the individual is a substantial part of self-realization. In your self-work you must be particularly alert to pay attention to the two principles. True spirituality must make fuller men and women out of you in the best sense, on all levels of your being. Your growth must inevitably harmonize these levels. In what way and to what degree the imbalance exists varies in each case and must be found individually by self-search.

When you become capable of truly loving, these principles will be perfectly expressed in you. Or, to put it the other way, *through the deliberate activation of the creative power to its highest potential because you no longer fear your own destructiveness and trust the universal powers to complete lawfully what you have deliberately set in motion, you will be unafraid to surrender to a power greater than your willful ego-self, and thus become capable of loving.* Whatever you do then in this spirit will be creative and will combine these two aspects of creation. The desire to give to life will never be threatened by self-impoverishment—on the contrary. The loving man will activate a sublime power in himself and his mate for the purpose of enriching them both. Her trust in him will be warranted, making her self-surrender justified and dignified, and enhancing her individuality. Giving up her determining ego will be for her a desired experience that need not be feared; his activation then becomes lovingly enriching to both. This is quite different from the kind of activating the pseudo-masterful man issues forth. He has an attitude that puts the woman down to aggrandize himself and makes her fear of surrender justified and reasonable. He therefore hinders her fulfillment as a woman.

The surrender of the loving woman heightens the mastery of self-activation in her mate. She will encourage his full selfhood, not competing with his activation because it no longer is a threat. Her receptivity should not be confused with the paralyzed passivity which is but a distortion of healthy femininity. The pulsating activity of the soul in the receptive state of letting-be, the state of being, self-surrender, is a vibrating force that contributes to her mate's manhood and to his strength.

When the letting-go is a deliberate choice to forgo the active principle at a certain point because the person recognizes that other faculties must now take over, an enormous difference is experienced. *The activating principle of becoming* causes things to happen deliberately; *the being principle* is self-perpetuating and involuntary; its effects occur indirectly.

The Pathwork itself requires blending of these two aspects. I wish to show you right here how it works.

No obstruction can be removed, no unhappiness eliminated, unless the personality, be it man or woman, uses the activating power. It is necessary to deliberately turn on this power by claiming your potential and your right to become a happy person. Nor must one shy away from the effort of finding the cause of the unhappiness within oneself. In other words, a person must be moving in the direction of correcting the errors within and at the same time deliberately calling upon a higher wisdom and power deep within the self to make this endeavor meaningful. The mind issues the will and determines the steps, as well as calls upon a greater wisdom within. All these are truly activities, each in its own fashion. But after these steps, the receptive principle must be at work, because once these forces have been activated, the entity has to let them come to fruition. The person who cannot wait for this to happen, but wants immediate results and attributes them solely to his activation, violates the feminine principle of the particular creation. Thus the creation will not be successful, or will succeed only to the degree to which the two creative aspects were able to function. A seed sown into the soil cannot at once be pulled out as a plant. It must be given time to grow within the earth until the first shoots appear. Agricultural laws demonstrate beautifully the wholeness of the two aspects of creation. The Pathwork is such a purposeful creative act, using the two principles in equal measure.

Be blessed, my friends, every one of you. May you find new strength and new stimulation from these words and a new opening of doors to help you where you may have been stuck. Perhaps my words will find an echo in your heart that will set something in motion within you which may make you want to activate more your search in the direction that leads deep into yourself. After facing, accepting, understanding, and eliminating the obstructions, your highest creative powers can begin to unfold. Be blessed, bring forth more and more the greatness and the beauty that you inherently are—God!

The Forces of
Love, Eros, and Sexuality

Greetings and blessings for all of you here, my dearest friends. Blessed is this hour.

Tonight I would like to discuss three particular forces in the universe: the love force as it manifests between the sexes, the erotic force, and the sexual force. These are three distinctly different principles or forces that manifest differently on every plane, from the highest to the lowest. Humanity has always confused these three principles. In fact, it is little known that three separate forces exist and what the differences between them are. There is so much confusion about this that it will be quite useful to clear them up.

The Spiritual Meaning of the Erotic Force

The erotic force is one of the most potent forces in existence and has tremendous momentum and impact. It is supposed to serve as the bridge between sex and love, yet it rarely does. In a spiritually highly developed person, the erotic force carries the entity from the erotic experience, which in itself is of short duration, into the permanent state of pure love. However, even the strong momentum of the erotic force carries the soul just so far and no farther. It is bound to dissolve if the personality does not learn to love by cultivating all the qualities and requirements necessary for true love. Only when love has been learned does the spark of the erotic force remain alive.

By itself, without love, the erotic force burns itself out. This of course is the trouble with marriage. Since most people are incapable of pure love, they are also incapable of attaining ideal marriage.

Eros seems in many ways similar to love. It brings forth impulses a human being would not have otherwise: impulses of unselfishness and affection he or she might have been incapable of before. This is why eros is so very often confused with love. But eros is just as often confused with the sex instinct which, like eros, also manifests as a great urge.

Now, my friends, I would like to show you what the spiritual meaning and purpose of the erotic force is, particularly as far as humanity is concerned. Without eros, many people would never experience the great feeling and beauty that is contained in real love. They would never get the taste of it and the yearning for love would remain deeply submerged in their souls. Their fear of love would remain stronger than their desire.

Eros is the nearest thing to love the undeveloped spirit can experience. It lifts the soul out of sluggishness, out of mere contentment and vegetation. It causes the soul to surge, to go out of itself. When this force comes upon even the most undeveloped people they become able to surpass themselves. Even a criminal will temporarily feel, at least toward one person, a goodness he has never known. The utterly selfish person will, while this feeling lasts, have unselfish impulses. Lazy people will get out of their inertia. The routine-bound person will naturally and without effort get rid of static habits. The erotic force will lift a person out of separateness, be it only for a short time. Eros gives the soul a foretaste of unity and teaches the fearful psyche the longing for it. The more strongly one has experienced eros, the less contentment will the soul find in the pseudo-security of separateness. Even an otherwise thoroughly self-centered person may be able to make a sacrifice during the experience of eros. So you see, my friends, eros enables people to do things they are disinclined to do otherwise; things that are closely linked with love. It is easy to see why eros is so often confused with love.

The Difference Between Eros and Love

How then is eros different from love? Love is a permanent state in the soul; eros is not. Love can only exist if the foundation for it is prepared through development and purification. Love does not come and go at random; eros does. Eros hits with sudden force, often taking a person unawares and even finding him or her unwilling to go through the experience. Only if the soul is prepared to love and has built the foundation for it will eros be the bridge to the love that is manifest between a man and a woman.

Thus you can see how important the erotic force is. Without the erotic force hitting them and getting them out of their rut, many human beings would never be ready for a more conscious search for the breaking down of their own walls of separation. The erotic experience puts the seed into the soul and makes it long for unity, which is the great aim in the plan of salvation. As long as the soul is separate, loneliness and unhappiness must be its lot. The erotic experience enables the personality to long for union with at least one other being. In the heights of the spirit world, union exists among all beings—and thus with God. In the earth sphere, the erotic force is a propelling power regardless of whether or not its real meaning is understood. This is so even though it is often misused and enjoyed for its own sake, while it lasts. It is not utilized to cultivate love in the soul, so it peters out. Nevertheless, its effect will inevitably remain in the soul.

The Fear of Eros and the Fear of Love

Eros comes to people suddenly in certain stages of their lives, even to those who are afraid of the apparent risk of adventuring away from separateness. People who are afraid of their emotions and afraid of life as such will often do anything in their power to avoid—unconsciously and ignorantly—the great experience of unity. Although this fear exists in many human beings, there are few indeed who have not experienced some opening in the soul where eros could touch them. For the fear-ridden soul that resists the experience, this is good medicine regardless of the fact that sorrow and loss may follow due to other psychological complications. However, there are also those who are overemotional, and although they may know other fears of life, they are not afraid of this particular experience. In fact, the beauty of it is a great temptation to them and therefore they hunt greedily for it. They look for one subject after another, emotionally too ignorant to understand the deep meaning of eros. They are unwilling to learn pure love, and simply use the erotic force for their pleasure and when it is worn out they hunt elsewhere. This is an abuse and cannot continue without ill effects. Such a personality will have to make amends for the abuse—even if it was done in ignorance. In the same vein, the too fearful coward will have to make up for trying to cheat life by hiding from eros and thus withholding from the soul a valuable medicine, valuable if used properly. Most people in this category have a vulnerable point somewhere in their soul through which eros can enter.

There are also a few who have built such a tight wall of fear and pride around their souls that they avoid this part of life-experience entirely and so shortchange their own development. This fear might exist because in a former life they had an unhappy experience with eros, or perhaps because the soul has greedily abused the beauty of the erotic force without building it into love. In either case, the personality may have chosen to be more careful. If this decision is too rigid and stringent, the opposite extreme will follow. In the next incarnation circumstances will be chosen in such a way that a balance is established until the soul reaches a harmonious state wherein there are no more extremes. This balancing in future incarnations always applies to all aspects of the personality. In order to approach this harmony to some extent at least, the proper balance between reason, emotion, and will has to be achieved.

The erotic experience often mingles with the sexual urge, but it does not always have to be that way. These three forces— love, eros, and sexuality—often appear completely separately, while sometimes two mingle, such as *eros and sexuality,* or *eros and love* to the extent the soul is capable of love, or *sexuality and a semblance of love.* Only in the ideal case do all three forces mingle harmoniously.

The Sexual Force

The sexual force is the creative force on any level of existence. In the highest spheres, the same force creates spiritual life, spiritual ideas, and spiritual concepts and principles. On the lower planes, the pure and unspiritualized sex force creates life as it manifests in that particular sphere; it creates the outer shell or vehicle of the entity destined to live in that sphere.

The pure sexual force is utterly selfish. *Sex without eros and without love* is referred to as animalistic. Pure sex exists in all living creatures: animals, plants, and minerals. Eros begins with the stage of development where the soul is incarnated as a human being. And pure love is to be found in the higher spiritual realms. This does not mean that eros and sex no longer exist in beings of higher development, but rather that all three blend in harmoniously, are refined, and become less and less selfish. Nor do I mean that a human being should not try to achieve a harmonious blend of all three forces.

In rare cases, *eros alone, without sex and love,* exists for a limited time. This is usually referred to as platonic love. But sooner or later, with the somewhat healthy person, eros and sex will mingle. The sex force, instead of being suppressed, is taken up by the erotic force and both flow in one current. The more the three forces remain separate, the unhealthier the personality is.

Another frequent combination, particularly in relationships of long standing, is the coexistence of genuine *love with sex, but without eros.* Although love cannot be perfect unless all three forces blend together, there is a certain amount of affection, companionship, fondness, mutual respect, and a sex-relationship that is crudely sexual without the erotic spark which evaporated some time ago. When eros is missing, the sexual relationship must eventually suffer. Now this is the problem with most marriages, my friends. There is hardly a human being who is not puzzled by the question of what to do to maintain that spark in a relationship which seems to evaporate the more habit and familiarity with one another sets in. You may not have posed the question in terms of three distinct forces, yet you know and sense that something goes out of a marriage that was present at the beginning; that spark is actually eros. You find yourself in a vicious circle and think that marriage is a hopeless proposition. No, my friends, it is not, even if you cannot as yet attain the ideal.

The Ideal Partnership of Love

In the ideal partnership of love between two people all three forces have to be represented. With love you do not seem to have much difficulty, for in most cases one would not marry if there did not exist at least the willingness to love. I will not discuss at this point the extreme cases where this is not so. I am focusing on a relationship where the choice is a mature one and yet the partners cannot get around the pitfall of becoming bound by time and habit, because *elusive eros has disappeared.* With sex it is very much the same. The sex force is present in most healthy human beings and may only begin to fade—particularly with women—when eros has left. Men may then seek eros elsewhere. For the sexual relationship must eventually suffer unless eros is maintained.

How can you keep eros? That is the big question, my dear ones. Eros can be maintained only if it is used as a bridge to true partnership in love in the highest sense. How is this done?

The Search for the Other Soul

Let us first look for the main element in the erotic force. When you analyze it, you will find that it is the adventure, the search for the knowledge of the other soul. This desire lives in every created spirit. The inherent life-force must finally bring the entity out of its separation. Eros strengthens the curiosity to know the other being. As long as there is something new to find in the other soul and as long as you reveal yourself, eros will live. The moment you believe you have found all there is to find, and have revealed all there is to reveal, eros will leave. It is as simple as that with eros. But your great error is that you believe there is a limit to the revealing of any soul, yours or another's. When a certain point of usually quite superficial revelation is reached, you are under the impression that this is all there is, and you settle down to a placid life without further searching.

Eros has carried you this far with its strong impact. But after this point, your will to further search the unlimited depths of the other person and voluntarily reveal and share your own inward search determines whether you have used *eros as a bridge to love*. This, in turn, is always determined by your will to learn how to love. Only in this way will you maintain the spark of eros in your love. Only in this way will you continue to *find the other and let yourself be found*. There is no limit, for the soul is endless and eternal: a whole lifetime would not suffice to know it.

There can never be a point when you know the other soul entirely, nor when you are known entirely. The soul is alive, and nothing that is alive remains static. It has the capacity to reveal even deeper layers. The soul is also in constant change and movement as anything spiritual is by its very nature. Spirit means life and life means change. Since soul is spirit, the soul can never be known utterly. If people had the wisdom, they would realize that and make of marriage the marvelous journey of adventure it is supposed to be, instead of simply being carried as far as you are taken by the first momentum of eros. You should use this potent momentum of eros as the initial thrust it is, and then find through it the urge to go on further under your own steam. Then you will have brought eros into true love in marriage.

The Pitfalls of Marriage

Behind the institution of marriage there is a divine intent, and its purpose is not merely procreation. That is only one detail. The spiritual idea of marriage is to enable the soul to reveal itself and to be constantly on the search for the other to discover forever new vistas of the other being. The more this happens, the happier the marriage will be, the more firmly and safely it will be rooted, and the less it will be in danger of an unhappy ending. Then it will fulfill its spiritual purpose.

In practice, however, marriage hardly ever works that way. You reach a certain state of familiarity and habit and you think you know the other. It does not even occur to you that the other only knows certain facets of your being, but that is all. This search for the other being, as well as for self-revelation, requires inner activity and alertness. But since people are often tempted into inner inactivity, while outer activity may be all the stronger as an overcompensation, they are being lured to sink into a state of restfulness, cherishing the delusion of already knowing each other fully. This is the pitfall. It is the beginning of the end at worst, or at best a compromise leaving you with a gnawing, unfulfilled longing. At this point the relationship turns static. It is no longer alive even though it may have some very pleasant features. Habit is a great temptress, pulling one toward sluggishness and inertia, so that one does not have to try and work or be alert anymore.

Two people may arrange an apparently satisfactory relationship, and as the years go by they face two possibilities. The first is that either one or both partners become openly and consciously dissatisfied. For the soul needs to surge ahead, to find and to be found, so as to dissolve separateness, regardless of how much the other side of the personality fears union and is tempted by inertia. This dissatisfaction is either conscious—although in most instances the *real* reason for it is ignored—or it is unconscious. In either case, the dissatisfaction is stronger than the temptation of the comfort of inertia and sluggishness. Then the marriage will be disrupted and one or both partners will delude themselves into thinking that with a new partner it will be different, particularly after eros has perhaps struck again. As long as this principle is not understood, a person may go from one partnership to another, sustaining feelings only as long as eros is at work.

The second possibility is that the temptation of a semblance of peace is stronger. Then the partners may remain together and may certainly fulfill something together, but a great unfulfilled need will always lurk in their souls. Since men are by nature more active and adventurous, they tend to be polygamous and are therefore more tempted by infidelity than women. Thus you can also understand what the underlying motive for men's inclination to be unfaithful is. Women tend much more to be sluggish and are therefore better prepared to compromise. This is why they tend to be monogamous. Of course, there are exceptions, in both sexes. Such infidelity is often as puzzling to the active partner as to the "victim." They do not understand themselves. The unfaithful one may suffer just as much as the one whose trust has been betrayed.

In the situation where *compromise* is chosen, both people stagnate, at least in one very important aspect of their soul development. They find refuge in the steady comfort of their relationship. They may even believe that they are happy in it, and this may be true to some degree. The advantages of friendship, companionship, mutual respect, and a pleasant life together with a well-established routine outweigh the unrest of the soul, and the partners may have enough discipline to remain faithful to one another. Yet an important element of their relationship is missing: the revealing of soul to soul as much as possible.

True Marriage

Only when two people do this can they be *purified together* and thus help each other. Two developed souls can fulfill one another by revealing themselves, by searching the depths of the other's soul. Thus what is in each soul will emerge into their conscious minds, and purification will take place. Then the life spark is maintained so that the relationship can never stagnate and degenerate into a dead end. For you who are on this path and follow the various steps of these teachings, it will be easier to overcome the pitfalls and dangers of the marital relationship and to repair damage that has occurred unwittingly.

In this way, my dear friends, you not only maintain eros, that vibrating life-force, but you also transform it into true love. Only in a true partnership of love and eros can you discover in your partner new levels of being you have not heretofore perceived. And you yourself will be purified also by putting away your pride and revealing yourself as you really are. Your relationship will always be new, regardless of how well you think you know each other already. All masks must fall, not only those on the surface, but even those deeper down which you may not even have been aware of. Then your love will remain alive. It will never be static; it will never stagnate. You will never have to search elsewhere. There is so much to see and discover in this land of the other soul you have chosen, whom you continue to respect, but in whom you seem to miss the life-spark that once brought you together. You will never have to be afraid of losing the love of your beloved; this fear will be justified only if you refrain from risking the journey of self-revelation together. This, my friends, *is marriage in its true sense*, and this is the only way it can be the glory it is supposed to be.

Separateness

Each of you should think deeply about whether you are afraid to leave the four walls of your own separateness. Some of my friends are unaware that to stay separate is almost a conscious wish. With many of you it is this way: you desire marriage because one part of you yearns for it—and also because you do not want to be alone. Quite superficial and vain reasons may be added to explain the deep yearning within your soul. But aside from the yearning and aside from the superficial and selfish motives of your unfulfilled desire for partnership, there must also be an unwillingness to risk the journey and adventure of revealing yourself. An integral part of life remains to be fulfilled by you—if not in this life, then in future lives.

Should you find yourself alone, you may, with this knowledge and this truth, repair the damage that you have done to your own soul by harboring wrong concepts in your unconscious. You may discover your fear of the great adventurous journey with another, which will explain why you are alone. This understanding should prove helpful and may even enable your emotions to change sufficiently so that your outer life may change too. This depends on you. Whoever is unwilling to take the risk of this great adventure cannot succeed in the greatest venture humanity knows—marriage.

Choice of Partner
Only when you meet love, life, and the other being in such readiness will you be able to bestow the greatest gift on your beloved, namely your true self. And then you must inevitably receive the same gift from your beloved. But to do that, a certain emotional and *spiritual maturity* has to exist. If this maturity is present, you will intuitively choose the right partner, one who has, in essence, the same maturity and readiness to embark on this journey. The choice of a partner who is unwilling comes out of the hidden fear of undertaking the journey yourself. *You magnetically draw people and situations toward you which correspond to your unconscious desires and fears.* You know that.

Humanity, on the whole, is very far away from this ideal of the marriage of true selves, but that does not change the idea or the ideal. In the meantime you have to learn to make the best of it. And you who are fortunate enough to be on this path can learn much wherever you stand, be it only in understanding why you cannot realize the happiness that a part of your soul yearns for. To discover that is already a great deal and will enable you in this life or in future lives to get nearer to the realization of what you yearn for. Whatever your situation is, whether you have a partner or are alone, search your heart and it will furnish you the answer to your conflict. The answer must come from within yourself, and in all probability it will relate to your own fear, unwillingness, and your ignorance of the facts. Search and you will know. Understand that God's purpose in the partnership of love is the *complete* mutual revelation of one soul to another—not just a partial revelation.

Physical revelation is easy for many. Emotionally you share to a certain degree—usually as far as eros carries you. But then you lock the door, and that is the moment when your troubles begin.

There are many who are not willing to reveal anything. They want to remain alone and aloof. They will not touch the experience of revealing themselves and of finding the soul of the other person. They avoid this in every way they can.

Eros As a Bridge

My dear ones, once again: understand how important the erotic principle is in your sphere. It helps many who may be unwilling and unprepared for the love-experience. It is what you call "falling in love," or "romance." Through eros the personality gets a taste of what the ideal love could be. As I said before, many use this feeling of happiness carelessly and greedily, never passing the threshold into true love. True love demands much more of people in a spiritual sense. If they do not meet this demand, they forfeit the goal for which their soul strives. This extreme of hunting for romance is as wrong as the other, where not even the potent force of eros can enter the tightly locked door. But in most cases, when the door is not too tightly bolted, eros does come to you at certain stages of your life. Whether you can then use eros as a bridge to love depends on you. It depends on your development, your willingness, your courage, your humility, and your ability to reveal yourself. Are there any questions in connection with this subject, my dear friends?

QUESTION: When you talk about the revelation of a soul to another, do you mean that, on a higher level, this is the way the soul reveals itself to God?

ANSWER: It is the same thing. But before you can truly reveal yourself to God, you have to learn to reveal yourself to another beloved human being. And when you do that, you reveal yourself to God too. Many people want to start with revealing themselves to the personal God. But actually, deep in their hearts, such revelation to God is only a subterfuge because it is abstract and remote. No other human being can see or hear what they reveal. They are still alone. One does not have to do the one thing that seems so risky, requires so much humility and thus threatens to be humiliating. By revealing yourself to another human being, you accomplish so much that cannot be accomplished by revelation to God who knows you anyway, and who really does not need your revelation.

When you find the other soul and meet it, you fulfill your destiny. When you find another soul, you also find another particle of God, and if you reveal your own soul, you reveal a particle of God and give something divine to another person. When eros comes to you, it will lift you up far enough so that you will sense and know what it is in you that longs for this experience and what is your true self, which is longing to reveal itself. Without eros, you are merely aware of the lazy outer layers.

Do not avoid eros when it wants to come to you. If you understand the spiritual idea behind it, you will use it wisely. Your Godself will then be able to lead you and enable you to make the best of helping another being and yourself on the way to true love, of which purification must be an integral part. Although your purification work through a deeply committed relationship manifests differently than it does in the work on this path, it will help you toward a purification of the same order.

QUESTION: Is it possible for a soul to be so rich that it can reveal itself to more than one soul?

ANSWER: My dear friend, do you say that facetiously?

QUESTION: No, I do not. I am asking whether polygamy is

within the scheme of spiritual law.

ANSWER: No, it certainly is not. And when someone thinks it may be within the scheme of spiritual development, that is a subterfuge. The personality is looking for the right partner. Either the person is too immature to have found the right partner, or the right partner is there and the polygamous person is simply carried away by eros's momentum, never lifting this force up into the volitional love that demands overcoming and working in order to pass the threshold I mentioned before.

In cases like this, the one with an adventurous personality is looking and looking, always finding another part of a being, always revealing himself or herself only so far and no further, or perhaps each time revealing another facet of his or her personality. However, when it comes to the inner nucleus, the door is shut. Eros then departs and a new search is started. Each time it is a disappointment that can only be understood when you grasp these truths.

Raw sexual instinct also enters into the longing for this great journey, but sexual satisfaction begins to suffer if the relationship is not kept on the level I show you here. It is, in fact, inevitably of short duration. There is no richness in revealing oneself to many. In such cases, one either reveals the same wares all over again to new partners, or, as I said before, one displays different facets of one's personality. The more partners you try to share yourself with, the less you give to each. That is inevitably so. It cannot be different.

QUESTION: Certain people believe that they can cut out sex and eros and the desire for a partner and live completely for love of humanity. Do you think it is possible that man or woman can swear off this part of life?

ANSWER: It is possible, but it is certainly not healthy or honest. I might say that there is perhaps one person in ten million who may have such a task. That may be possible. It may be in the karma for a particular soul who is already developed this far, has gone through the true partnership experience, and comes for a specific mission. There may also be certain karmic debts which have to be paid off. In most cases—and here I can safely generalize—avoidance of partnership is unhealthy. It is an escape. The real reason is fear of love, fear of the life experience, but the fearful renunciation is rationalized as a sacrifice. To anyone who would come to me with such a problem, I would say, "Examine yourself. Go below the surface layers of your conscious reasoning and explanations for your attitude in this respect. Try to find out whether you fear love and disappointment. Isn't it more comfortable to just live for yourself and have no difficulties? Isn't really this what you feel deep inside and what you want to cover up with other reasons? The great humanitarian work you want to do may be for a worthy cause indeed, but do you really think one excludes the other? Wouldn't it be much more likely that the great task you have taken upon yourself would be better fulfilled if you learned personal love too?"

If all these questions were truthfully answered, the person would be bound to see that he or she is escaping. Personal love and fulfillment is man's and woman's destiny in most cases, for so much can be learned in personal love that cannot be attained in any other way. And to form a durable and solid relationship in a marriage is the greatest victory a human being can achieve, for it is one of the most difficult things there is, as you can well see in your world. This life experience will bring the soul closer to God than lukewarm good deeds.

QUESTION: I was going to ask a question in connection with my previous one: celibacy is supposed to be a highly spiritualized form of development in certain religious sects. On the other hand, polygamy is also recognized in some religions—the Mormons, for instance. I understand what you said, but how do you justify these attitudes on the part of people who are supposed to look for unity with God?

ANSWER: There is human error in every religion. In one religion it may be one kind of error, in other religions another. Here you simply have two extremes. When such dogmas or rules come into existence in the various religions, whether at one extreme or another, it is always a rationalization and subterfuge to which the individual soul constantly resorts. This is an attempt to explain away the counter-currents of the fearful or greedy soul with good motives.

There is a common belief that anything pertaining to sexuality is sinful. This is not so. The sex instinct arises already in the infant. The more immature the creature, the more sexuality is separated from love, and therefore the more selfish it is. Anything without love is "sinful," if you want to use this word. Nothing that is coupled with love is wrong—or sinful.

In the growing child who is naturally immature, the sex drive will first manifest selfishly. Only if and when the whole personality grows and matures harmoniously will sex become integrated with love. Out of ignorance, humanity has long believed that sex as such is sinful. Therefore it was kept hidden and this part of the personality could not grow up. Nothing that remains in hiding can grow; you know that. Therefore, even in many grownups, sex remains childish and separate from love. And this, in turn, has led humanity to believe that sexuality is a sin and that the truly spiritual person must abstain from it. Thus one of those oft-mentioned vicious circles came into existence.

Because of the belief that sex was sinful, the instinct could not grow and meld with the love force. Consequently, sex in fact often is selfish and loveless, raw and animalistic. If people would realize—and they are beginning to do so increasingly— that the sex instinct is as natural and God-given as any other universal force and in itself not more sinful than any other existing force, they would break this vicious circle and more human beings would let their sex drives mature and mingle with love—and with eros, for that matter.

How many people exist for whom sex is completely separate from love! They not only suffer from bad conscience when the sex urge manifests, but they also find themselves in the position of being unable to handle sexual feelings with the person they really love. Because of the distorted conditions and the vicious circle just described, humanity came to believe that you cannot find God when you respond to your sex urges. This is all wrong; you cannot kill off something that is alive. You can only hide it so that it will come out in other ways which may be much more harmful. Only in the very rarest cases does the sex force really become constructively sublimated and make this creative force manifest in other realms. Real sublimation can never occur when it is motivated by fear and used as an escape. Does that answer your question?

QUESTION: Perfectly, thank you.

QUESTION: How does friendship between two people fit into this picture?

ANSWER: Friendship is brotherly love. Such friendship can also exist between man and woman. Eros may want to sneak in, but reason and will can still direct the way in which the feelings take their course. Discretion, and a healthy balance between reason, emotion, and will are necessary to prevent the feelings from going into an improper channel.

QUESTION: Is divorce against spiritual law?

ANSWER: Not necessarily. We do not have fixed rules like that. There are cases when divorce is an easy way out, a mere escape. There are other cases when divorce is reasonable because the choice to marry was made in immaturity and both partners lack the desire to fulfill the responsibility of marriage in its true sense. If only one is willing—or neither—divorce is better than staying together and making a farce out of marriage. Unless both are willing to take this journey together, it is better to break clean than to let one prevent the growth of the other. That, of course, happens. It is better to terminate a mistake than to remain indefinitely in it without finding an effective remedy.

To generalize that divorce is always wrong is just as incorrect as to say that it is always right. One should not, however, leave a marriage lightly. Even though it was a mistake and does not work, one should try to find the reasons and do one's very best to search out and perhaps get over the hurdles that are in the way, if both are in any way willing. One should certainly do one's best, even if the marriage is not the ideal experience that I discussed tonight. Few people are ready and mature enough for it. You can make yourself ready by trying to make the best of your past mistakes and learn from them.

My dearest friends, think carefully about what I have said. There is much food for thought in what I told you for each of you here, and for all those who will read my words. There is not a single person who cannot learn something from them.

My dear ones, receive our blessings again; may your hearts be filled with this wonderful strength coming to you from the world of light and truth. Go in peace and in happiness, my dear ones, each one of you. Be in God!

CHAPTER 4

The Spiritual Significance of Relationship

Greetings, my dearest, dearest friends. Blessings for every one of you. Blessed be your very life, your every breath, your thoughts and your feelings.

This lecture deals with relationships and their tremendous significance from the spiritual point of view—that of individual growth and unification. First, I would like to point out that on the human level of manifestation individual units of consciousness do exist, which sometimes harmonize, but very often conflict with one another, creating friction and crisis. Yet behind this level of manifestation there are no fragmented units of consciousness. There is only one consciousness, of which every single created entity is but a different expression. When one comes into one's own, one experiences this truth, without, however, losing a sense of individuality. This can be felt very distinctly when you deal with your own inner disharmonies, my friends. For there, too, exactly the same principle applies.

Unequal Development of Parts of Consciousness

In your present state, a part of your innermost being is developed and governs your thinking, feeling, willing, and acting. There are other parts, still in a lower state of development, which also govern and influence your thinking, feeling, willing and acting. Thus you find yourself divided, and this always creates tension, pain, anxiety, as well as inner and outer difficulties. Some aspects of your personality are in truth, others, in error and distortion. The resulting confusion causes grave disturbances. What you usually do is push one side out of the way and identify with the other. Yet the denial of a part of you cannot bring unification. On the contrary, it widens the split. What must be done is to bring out the deviating, conflicting side and face it—face the entire ambivalence. Only then do you find the ultimate reality of your unified self. As you know, unification and peace emerge to the degree you recognize, accept, and understand the nature of the inner conflict.

Exactly the same law applies to the unity or dissension between outwardly separate and different entities. They, too, are one, beyond the level of appearance. The dissension is caused not by actual differences among units of consciousness, but, just as in the individual, by differences in the development of the manifesting universal consciousness.

Even though *the principle of unification* is exactly the same within and among individuals, it *cannot be applied to another human being unless it has first been applied to one's inner self.* If the divergent parts of your self are not approached according to this truth, and your ambivalence is not faced, accepted, and understood, the process of unification cannot be put into practice with another person. *This is a very important fact, which explains the great emphasis of the Pathwork on first approaching the self.* Only then can relationship be cultivated in a meaningful and effective way.

Elements of Dissension and Unification

Relationship represents the greatest challenge for the individual, for it is only in relationship to others that unresolved problems still existing within the individual psyche are affected and activated. Many individuals withdraw from interaction with others, so they can maintain the illusion that the problems arise from the other person because one feels disturbance only in his or her presence, and not when by oneself.

However, the less contact is cultivated, the more acute the longing for contact becomes. This, then, is a different kind of pain—*the pain of loneliness and frustration.* But contact makes it difficult to maintain the illusion for any length of time that the inner self is faultless and harmonious. It requires mental aberration to claim for too long that one's problems in relationship are caused only by others and not by oneself. This is why relationships are simultaneously a fulfillment, a challenge, and a gauge to one's inner state. *The friction that arises out of relating with others can be a sharp instrument of purification and self-recognition* if one is inclined to use it.

By withdrawing from this challenge and sacrificing the fulfillment of intimate contact, many inner problems are never called into play. The illusion of inner peace and unity that comes from avoidance of relating has even led to concepts that spiritual growth is furthered by isolation. Nothing could be farther from the truth. This statement must not be confused with the notion that intervals of seclusion are necessary for inner concentration and self-confrontation. But these periods should always alternate with contact—and the more intimate such contact is, the more it expresses spiritual maturity.

Contact and lack of contact with others can be observed in various stages. There are many degrees of contact between the crass extremes of total outer and inner isolation, at one end, and the deepest, most intimate relatedness at the other. There are those who have obtained a certain superficial ability to relate but who still withdraw from a more meaningful, open, unmasked mutual revealing. I might say that the average present-day human being fluctuates somewhere between the two extremes.

Fulfillment as Yardstick for Personal Development

It is also possible to measure one's personal sense of fulfillment by the depth of relatedness and intimate contact, by the strength of the feelings one permits oneself to experience, and by the willingness to give and receive. Frustration indicates an absence of contact, which, in turn, is a precise indicator that the self withdraws from the challenge of relationship, thereby sacrificing personal fulfillment, pleasure, love, and joy. When you want to share only on the basis of receiving according to your own terms, and you are in fact secretly unwilling to share, your longings must remain unfulfilled. People would be well advised to consider their unfulfilled longings from this point of view, rather than indulging in the usual assumption that one is unlucky and unfairly put upon by life.

One's contentment and fulfillment in relationship is a much neglected yardstick for one's own development. Relationship with others is a mirror of one's own state and thus a direct help to one's self-purification. Conversely, only by thorough self-honesty and self-facing can relationships be sustained, can feelings expand and contact blossom in long-term relationships. So you can see, my friends, that relationships represent a tremendously important aspect of human growth.

The power and significance of relationship often pose severe problems for those who are still in the throes of their own inner conflicts. The unfulfilled longing becomes unbearably painful when isolation is chosen due to the difficulty of contact. This can be resolved only when you seriously settle down to *seek the cause for this conflict within your self,* without using the defense of annihilating guilt and self-blame, which of course eliminates any possibility of really getting at the core of the conflict. This search, together with the inner willingness to change, must be cultivated in order to escape the painful dilemma in which both available alternatives—isolation and contact—are unbearable.

It is important to remember that withdrawal can be very subtle and may be outwardly unnoticeable, manifesting only in a certain guardedness and distorted self-protection. Outer good fellowship does not necessarily imply a capacity and willingness for inner closeness. For many, closeness is too taxing. On the surface this seems related to how difficult others are, but actually the difficulty lies in the self, regardless of how imperfect others may also be.

Who is Responsible for the Relationship?

When people whose spiritual development is on different levels are involved with one another, *it is always the more highly developed person who is responsible for the relationship.*

Specifically, that person is responsible for searching the depths of the interaction which creates any friction and disharmony between the parties.

The less developed person is not as capable of such a search, being still in a state of blaming the other and depending on the other's doing "right" in order to avoid unpleasantness or frustration. Also, the less developed person is always caught up in *the fundamental error of duality.* From his or her perspective any friction is seen in terms of "only one of us is right." A problem in the other automatically seems to whitewash this person, although in reality his or her own negative involvement may be infinitely more weighty than the other person's.

The spiritually more developed person is capable of realistic, *non-dualistic perception.* That person may see that either one of you may have a deep problem, but that does not eliminate the importance of the possibly much lesser problem of the other one. The more developed one will always be willing and able to search for his or her own involvement whenever he or she is negatively affected, no matter how blatantly at fault the other may be. A person of spiritual and emotional immaturity and crudeness will always put the bulk of the blame on the other. All this applies to any kind of relationship: mates, parents and children, friendships, or business contacts.

The tendency to make yourself emotionally dependent on others—the overcoming of which is such an important aspect of the growth process—largely comes from wanting to absolve yourself from blame or extract yourself from difficulty when establishing and maintaining a relationship. It seems so much easier to shift most of this burden to others. But what a price to pay! Doing this renders you helpless indeed and brings about isolation, or unending pain and friction with others. It is only when you begin truly to assume self-responsibility by looking at your own problem in the relationship and show a willingness to change that freedom is established and relationships become fruitful and joyous.

If the more highly developed person refuses to undertake the appropriate spiritual duty to assume responsibility for the relationship and look for the core of dissension within, he or she will never really understand the mutual interaction, how one problem affects the other. The relationship must then deteriorate, leaving both parties confused and less able to cope with the self and others. On the other hand, if the spiritually developed person accepts this responsibility, he or she will also help the other in a subtle way. If he or she can desist from the temptation to constantly belabor the obvious sour points of the other and look within, he or she will raise his or her own development considerably and spread peace and joy. The poison of friction will soon be eliminated. It will also become possible to find other partners for a truly mutual growth process.

When two equals relate, both carry the full responsibility for the relationship. This is indeed a beautiful venture, a deeply satisfying state of mutuality. The slightest flaw in a mood will be recognized for its inner meaning and thus the growth process is kept up. Both will recognize their co-creation of this momentary flaw—be it an actual friction or a momentary deadness of feelings. The inner reality of the interaction will become increasingly more significant. This will largely prevent injury to the relationship.

Let me emphasize here that when I speak of being responsible for the less developed person, I do not mean that another human being can ever carry the burden for the actual difficulties of others. This can never be. What I mean is that difficulties of interaction in a relationship are usually not explored in depth by the individual whose spiritual development is more primitive. He or she will render others responsible for his or her unhappiness and disharmony in a given interaction and is not able, or willing, to see the whole issue. Thus that person is not in a position to eliminate the disharmony. Only those who assume responsibility for finding the inner disturbance and mutual effect can do so. Hence the spiritually more primitive person always depends on the spiritually more evolved one.

A relationship between individuals in which the destructiveness of the less developed one makes growth, harmony, and good feelings impossible, or in which the contact is overwhelmingly negative, should be severed. As a rule, the more highly developed person should assume the initiative. If he or she does not, this indicates some unrecognized weakness and fear that needs to be faced. If a relationship is dissolved on this ground, namely, that it is more destructive and pain-producing than constructive and harmonious, it should be done when the inner problems and mutual interactions are fully recognized by the one who takes the initiative to dissolve an old tie. This will prevent him or her from forming a new relationship with similar underlying currents and interactions. It also means that the decision to sever the connection has been made because of growth, rather than as a result of spite, fear, or escape.

Destructive Interactions

To explore the underlying interaction and the various effects of a relationship where both people's difficulties are laid bare and accepted is by no means easy. But nothing can be more beautiful and rewarding. Anyone who comes into the state of enlightenment where this is possible will no longer fear any kind of interaction. *Difficulties and fears arise to the exact degree that you still project on others your own problems* in relating and still render others responsible for anything that goes against your liking. This can take many subtle forms. You may constantly concentrate on the faults of others, because at first glance such concentration appears justified to you. You may subtly overemphasize one side of an interaction, or exclude another. Such distortions indicate projection and denial of self-responsibility for the difficulties in relating. This denial fosters *dependency on the perfection of the other party,* which in turn creates fear and hostility for feeling let down when the other does not measure up to the perfect standard.

My dear friends, no matter what wrong the other person does, if you are disturbed, there must be something in you that you overlook. When I say disturbed, I mean this in a particular sense. I do not speak of clear-cut anger that expresses itself guiltlessly and does not leave a trace of inner confusion and pain. I mean the kind of disturbance that comes out of conflict and breeds further conflict. A favorite tendency among people is to say, "You are doing it to me." *The game of making others guilty is so pervasive that you hardly even notice it.* One human being blames the other, one country blames the other, one group blames the other. This is a constant process at humanity's present level of development. *It is indeed one of the most harmful and illusory processes imaginable.*

People derive pleasure from doing this, although the pain that ensues and the insoluble conflicts that follow are infinitely disproportionate to the puny, momentary pleasure. Those who play this game truly harm themselves and others, and I strongly recommend that you begin to be aware of your blind involvement in this guilt-shifting game.

But how about the "victim"? How is that person to cope? As a victim, your first problem is that *you are not even aware of what is happening.* Most of the time, the victimization happens in a subtle, emotional, and unarticulated fashion. The silent, covert blame is being launched without a spoken word. It is expressed indirectly in many ways. Now, obviously, the first necessity is concise, articulate awareness, for otherwise you will unconsciously respond in equally destructive, falsely self-defensive ways. Then neither person really knows the intricate levels of action, reaction, and interaction until the threads become so enmeshed that it seems impossible to disentangle them. Many a relationship has faltered due to such unconscious interaction.

The *launching of blame spreads poison,* fear, and at least as much guilt as one tries to project. The recipients of this blame and guilt may react in many different ways, according to their own problems and unresolved conflicts. As long as the reaction is blind and the projection of guilt unconscious, the counter-reaction must also be neurotic and destructive. Only conscious perception can prohibit this. Only then will you be able to refuse a burden that is being placed on you. Only then can you articulate and pinpoint it.

How to Reach for Fulfillment and Pleasure

In a relationship that is about to blossom, one must be on the lookout for this pitfall, which is all the more difficult to detect because guilt projection is so widespread. Also, the recipients should look for it in themselves as well as in the other. I do not mean here a straightforward confrontation about something the other person did wrong. I mean the subtle blame for personal unhappiness. This is what must be challenged.

The only way you can avoid becoming a victim of blame and guilt projection is to avoid doing it yourself. To the degree you indulge yourself in this subtly negative attitude—and you may do it in a different way than the one who does it to you—you will be unaware of it being done to you and will therefore become victimized by it. The mere awareness will make all the difference—whether or not you verbally express your perception and confront the other person. Only to the degree that you undefensively explore and accept your own problematic reactions and distortions, negativities and destructiveness, can you defuse someone else's guilt projection. Only then will you not be drawn into a maze of falseness and confusion in which uncertainty, defensiveness, and weakness may make you either retreat or become overaggressive. Only then will you no longer confuse self-assertion with hostility, or flexible compromise with unhealthy submission.

These are the aspects which determine the ability to cope with relationships. The more profoundly understood and lived these new attitudes are, the more intimate, fulfilling, and beautiful human interaction will become.

How can you assert your rights and reach into the universe for fulfillment and pleasure? How can you love without fear unless you approach relating to others the way I have outlined above? Unless by learning to do this you purify yourself, there must always be a threat when it comes to intimacy: that one or both will resort to using the whip of loading guilt upon the other. Loving, sharing, and profound and satisfying closeness to others could be a purely positive power without any threat if these snares were looked at, discovered, and dissolved. It is of utmost importance that you look for them in yourselves, my friends.

The most challenging, beautiful, spiritually important and growth-producing kind of relationship is that between man and woman. The power that brings two people together in love and attraction, and the pleasure involved are a small aspect of being in cosmic reality. It is as though each created entity knew unconsciously about the bliss of this state and sought to realize it in the most potent way open to humanity: in love and sexuality between man and woman. The power that draws them together is the purest spiritual energy, leading to an inkling of the purest spiritual state.

When a man and a woman stay together in a more enduring and committed relationship, maintaining and even increasing bliss depends entirely on how the two relate to one another. Are they aware of the direct relationship between enduring pleasure and inner growth? Do they use the inevitable difficulties in the relationship as yardsticks for their own inner difficulties? Do they communicate in the deepest, most truthful, self-revealing way, sharing their inner problems, helping each other? The answers to these questions will determine whether the relationship falters, dissolves, stagnates—or blossoms.

When you look at the world around you, you will undoubtedly see that very few human beings grow and reveal themselves in such an open way. Equally few realize that *growing together and through each other* determines the solidity of feelings, of pleasure, of enduring love and respect. It is therefore not surprising that long-lasting relationships are almost invariably more or less dead in feelings.

Difficulties that arise in a relationship are always signals for something unattended to. They are a loud message for those who can hear it. The sooner it is heeded, the more spiritual energy will be released, so that the state of bliss can expand along with the inner being of both partners. There is a mechanism in a relationship between a man and a woman that can be likened to a very finely calibrated instrument that shows the finest and most subtle aspects of the relationship and the individual state of the two people involved. This is not sufficiently recognized by even the most aware and sophisticated people who are otherwise familiar with spiritual and psychological truth. Every day and every hour one's inner state and feelings are a testimony to one's state of growth. To the degree they are heeded, the interaction, the feelings, the freedom of flow within and toward each other will blossom.

The perfectly mature and spiritually valid relationship must always be deeply connected with personal growth. The moment a relationship is experienced as irrelevant to inner growth, left on its own, as it were, it will falter. Only when both grow to their ultimate, inherent potential can the relationship become more and more dynamic and alive. This work has to be done individually and mutually. When relationship is approached in that way, it will be built on rock, not sand. No fear will ever find room under such circumstances. Feelings will expand, and security about the self and each other will grow. At any given moment, each partner will serve as a mirror to the inner state of the other and therefore to the relationship.

Whenever there is friction or deadness, it is an indication that something must be stuck. Some interaction between the two people remains unclear and it needs to be looked at. If it is understood and brought out into the open, growth will proceed at maximum speed, and, in the dimension of feeling, happiness, bliss, profound experience, and ecstasy will become forever deeper and more beautiful, and life will acquire more meaning.

Conversely, fear of intimacy implies rigidity and the denial of one's own share in the relationship's difficulties. Anyone who ignores these principles, or who pays only lip service to them, is emotionally not ready to assume the responsibility for his or her inner suffering—either within a relationship or in its absence.

So you see, my friends, it is of the greatest importance to recognize that *bliss and beauty, which are eternal spiritual realities, are available to all those who seek the key to the problems of human interaction, as well as to loneliness, within their own hearts. True growth is as much a spiritual reality as are profound fulfillment, vibrant aliveness, and blissful, joyous relating.* When you are inwardly ready to relate to another human being in such a fashion, *you will find the appropriate partner* with whom this manner of sharing is possible. It will no longer frighten you, will no longer beset you with conscious or unconscious fears when you use this all-important key. You cannot ever feel helpless or victimized when the significant transition has taken place in your life and you no longer render others responsible for what you experience or fail to experience. Thus growth and fulfilled, beautiful living become one and the same.

May you all carry with you this new material and an inner energy awakened by your goodwill. May these words be the beginning of a new inner modality to meet life, to finally decide, "I want to risk my good feelings. I want to seek the cause in me, rather than in the other person, so that I become free to love." This kind of meditation will indeed bear fruit. If you carry away a germ, a particle, of this lecture, it has truly been fruitful. Be blessed, all of you, my dearest friends, so that you become the gods that you potentially are.

CHAPTER 5

Mutuality: A Cosmic Principle and Law

Greetings, my friends. Blessings and love for every one of you. The topic of tonight's lecture is mutuality. I will divide this subject into three sections: mutuality as a cosmic principle and law; how this law manifests in human life; and the nature and origin of the hindrances that upset the balance of mutuality.

No creation can take place unless mutuality exists. Mutuality means that two apparently or superficially different entities or aspects move toward one another for the purpose of uniting and making one comprehensive whole. They open up toward one another and cooperate with and affect one another so as to create a new divine manifestation. *New forms of self-expression can only come into being when the self merges with something beyond itself.* Mutuality is the movement that bridges the gap between duality and unity. Wherever there is separation, mutuality must come into being, in order to eliminate the separation.

Nothing can be created unless mutuality exists, be it a new galaxy, a work of art, or a good relationship between human beings. This applies even to the creation of the simplest object. First the idea of the object must be formed in the mind. Without the creative inspiration and imagination by which the mind extends itself beyond its previous awareness of what already exists, not even a plan can be made. The creative aspect must then cooperate with the second aspect of mutuality, namely execution, which implies labor, effort, perseverance, and self-discipline. The first aspect, creative thinking and inspiration, can never complete creation unless the second aspect, that of execution, is brought to the task.

Human beings are uncreative for two reasons: either they are unwilling to adopt the necessary self-discipline to follow through on their creative ideas, or they are emotionally and spiritually too contracted to open their own individual creative channels. When people begin to resolve their inner conflicts and become more healthy and balanced, they find their personal creative outlets that yield the deepest satisfaction.

Mutuality as a Bridge

An imbalance of the two aspects of creation is particularly striking in the area of *human relationships*. The movement that brings two people together in an initial attraction and love is creative, spontaneous, and effortless. Yet the connection is rarely maintained. What mostly happens is that the labor of working out the hidden inner dissensions is neglected. The childish idea prevails that the self is powerless to determine the course of the relationship. Usually the relationship is treated as if it were a separate entity that, either favorably or unfavorably, runs its own course.

Mutuality is the bridge that leads to unification. Two expansive movements must flow out toward one another in a harmonious interplay of giving and receiving, of mutual cooperation, of positive opening. Two "yes-currents"—manifestations of positive intent—must move toward one another. The ability to accept, bear, and sustain pleasure can be learned only gradually; it is one of the most difficult goals to reach. This ability depends directly on a person's spiritual and emotional wholeness. Hence, *mutuality depends on the entity's ability to say "yes" when a "yes" is offered.*

This brings us to the second section of this lecture.

How Does the Principle of Mutuality Apply to Humanity's Present State of Development?

There are three gradations.

The human being who is least developed and still full of fear and misconceptions is able to expand only very little. Since expansion and mutuality are interdependent, mutuality is impossible to the degree that expansion is denied. All human beings are afraid of opening up to some degree, as you well know. You may not suspect that such a fear exists in you. Or, if you do suspect it, you may explain it away because you are too ashamed to admit it. You may think that there is something especially wrong with you, something that no other valuable human being shared. Therefore no one must be allowed to suspect this flaw in you. But as you go on with your inner work, you learn to fully admit, accept, and properly understand the universality of your problem and can acknowledge your fear of opening up and expanding. You may at times be quite aware of this fear and see how you hold back your energy, your feelings, and your vital forces, because you believe yourself safer through this kind of control. To the degree that you do this, you will have problems with mutuality.

People who are the least developed and the most alienated from their inner truth will not be ready for any kind of expansion and therefore for any mutuality. However, this does not mean that their longing for it is eliminated; *the longing is always there.* Yet some entities manage to squelch their longing for expansion and mutuality perhaps through entire incarnations without becoming aware that so much is lacking in their lives. They content themselves with the pseudo-security of separateness and aloneness, for this offers less threat, or so it seems.

However, when development proceeds a little more, the longing becomes stronger and more conscious. There are many degrees and many alternatives. To oversimplify for the sake of clarity: *people at the second stage are willing to open up but are still afraid when an opportunity arises for actual mutuality. The only way the bliss and pleasure of expansion and union can be experienced for people at this stage is in fantasy.*

This leads to a very common and frequent fluctuation of experiences. People in this stage are convinced that their strong longing indicates that they are ready for real mutuality.

After all, they experience it so beautifully in their fantasies! That they still do not experience it in reality is attributed to their lack of luck in meeting the proper partner with whom they could realize these fantasies. When a partner finally appears, the old fear is still rampant. The soul movements contract and the fantasy cannot be realized. This is usually explained away by all sorts of outer circumstances, which may even be true. The partner may actually have too many obstructions to help them realize the dream. Yet, does this very fact not indicate that some deeper force must be at work in the person's psyche that makes sure to attract the partner with whom the contraction appears justified? For the deeper self always knows where a person stands. If the willingness is still lacking to face the deeper issues in truth, subterfuges and excuses are very necessary for the preservation of the ego. But failure in the relationship always indicates that the self is not yet ready to put true mutuality into practice.

Many people continue to go alternately through periods of aloneness and acute longing, then temporary fulfillment of a sort in which either outer or inner obstructions prevent full mutuality. The consequent disappointments may lend even more justification to unconscious fears which feed the resolve not to open up and be carried by the stream of life. The pain and the confusion is often very profound in people trapped at this stage. But this pain and confusion will eventually lead to more self-work and the full commitment to find the inner source of the fluctuation.

The meaning of this stage is rarely understood. The pain and confusion are there because the fluctuation's true significance is not recognized. When a growing person comes to see that periods of aloneness afford him or her some opportunity to open up in comparative safety and to experience, even though vicariously, some manner of fulfillment without taking the necessary risks, he or she has indeed made a substantial step toward self-realization. Concomitantly, when he or she recognizes the true underlying significance of the difficulties encountered during the times of tentative relationships, the same holds true. The alternating periods of aloneness and relating have their own built-in safety valves: each preserves the self in its separate state and simultaneously helps it venture out to the extent the entity has become ready to come out of separation.

At one point on the road of individual evolution, however, everyone comes to recognize fully how painful this fluctuation is, which subsequently leads to a commitment to be open to mutuality and fulfillment, to interplay and expansion, to cooperation and positive pleasure. This always requires relinquishing the negative pleasure of the pseudo-safety. The soul then becomes ready to learn, to experiment, risk mutuality, love, pleasure, and to function safely in an open state.

At the third stage are the people capable of sustaining mutuality in actuality—not in fantasy, not in longing only. Needless to say that all steady relationships on this earth do not indicate real mutuality. In fact, very, very few do. Most relationships are formed on other assumptions, or else the motivation of mutuality was originally there, but given up when it could not be maintained and was replaced by other ties.

These are basically the three stages humanity goes through with respect to mutuality. Of course, these stages cannot be differentiated in such exact terms. They often overlap, fluctuate and interchange; many degrees exist and hold true for each of the various levels of the personality. What may be true on one level for a specific person may not be true on another.

What Prohibits Mutuality Between Human Beings?

Now let us come to the third and perhaps most important part of this lecture. What are the obstacles prohibiting mutuality between two human beings? Usually this is explained, and quite accurately in part, by people's problems. Yet this does not really say enough.

Mutuality can exist only to the degree that individuals know about and are in contact with their previously hidden destructive sides. Conversely, if there is a rift between the *conscious* striving for goodness, love, and decency, and the *unconscious* bent on destructiveness, mutuality cannot take place. I emphasize that mutuality is absent not because the negative aspects are still there, but *because there is not sufficient awareness of them.* This is an all-important distinction. *Usually human beings approach this problem in precisely the opposite way. They believe that they must first eradicate the still existing evil, for otherwise they are undeserving of the bliss that comes from mutuality.* The inner evil is too frightening to be acknowledged, and therefore the rift between the conscious awareness of self and the unconscious denial of self widens as life goes on.

If you are alienated from your own unconscious, you must act out what deep in yourself you know exists within you. You act it out with another person and affect the unconscious and concealed level of that other person. Unless this key is applied, relationships must falter or become stale, and mutuality in the true sense cannot unfold. Therefore *it is crucial for you to gain increasing contact with the unconscious destructive aspects of your being.* How very difficult it seems for people to bridge the gap between the conscious good and the unconscious evil! How much struggle everyone puts up, and how many people are tempted to leave this pursuit altogether because it seems too painful and difficult to accept the previously unacceptable aspects of themselves. Yet life cannot be truly lived unless this happens.

The split between your conscious self and your real self that includes the unconscious aspects must reappear as a split between you and others unless you are fully conscious of the former. Becoming conscious of your real self is to begin mending this rift—consciousness diminishes the rift. Consciousness must eventually lead to accepting of what has previously been denied. If there is no mutuality between you and all aspects of yourself because your standards, your demands, and your expectations of yourself are unrealistic, it is absolutely unthinkable that mutuality between you and others can ever exist.

Mutuality between you and yourself is absent when you reject the evil within you. *Rejecting evil, you ignore and deny the vital, original creative energy that is contained in all evil.* This energy must be made available to you for you to become whole. The energy can only be transformed when you are aware of its distorted form: yet, when you reject its present manifestation, how can you reconvert it? Hence you remain split within yourself. And when the split is not conscious, it mirrors itself in your relationships—or in the lack of them. No matter how evil and unacceptable any specific trait in you may be, no matter how undesirable and destructive, the energy and substance it consists of is a vital force without which you cannot fully function. Only as a whole person can you sustain pleasure; only as a fully conscious person can you be whole. Only then can you not block the expansive movement and let yourself flow out into the universe of another entity, while remaining open to receive the other's outflowing energy currents and soul movements.

Keys for Your Inner Work

Your disunity with yourself cannot bring unity with others. It is utter folly to expect it. However, *you do not have to wait to become totally unified first.* If you take your ongoing relationships and use them as yardsticks by which you gauge where your own inner split is and where you stand in your willingness to accept the negative in you, you will grow into greater self-acceptance. Simultaneously, your ability to have mutuality will grow in proportion to your self-acceptance. Hence your relationships will improve and become much more deeply meaningful. The acceptance of whatever in you you have rejected because you refused to become conscious of it, will immediately produce a greater acceptance and understanding of other people you have to deal with. Mutuality will then become possible.

By the same token, if you cannot accept the evil in you, thinking, in effect, "I must first be perfect before I can accept, love, trust, esteem myself," you must express an identical attitude toward the other person. When the reality dawns on you that he or she is far from perfect, you reject the other person just as you keep rejecting your own self. The difference is that you manage most of the time not to know what you are doing with yourself. This is very unfortunate. You manage not to see the rejection of your own imperfect self and that of the other for what it is. You explain it away. This causes a rift in you that makes mutuality and bliss impossible.

All of you can use what I say here as a very practical and immediate key in your inner work. You can look at your relationships with your family, your partners, your associates, your friends, your business acquaintances. Look closely at any life situation where you are involved with others if anything troubles you about them. To what degree are you truly open to the reality of the other person? If you honestly answer this question, and you can see that you are not open, you can then use this key for yourself. Of course, you can easily shirk seeing it by busying yourself with your explanations, justifications, rationalizations—and even with your acute self-blame which may easily be confused with self-acceptance, but is just as far removed from it as is overt self-denial. On the deeper emotional levels you will see that in many instances the willingness to accept others as they are is very small. As you slowly discover your intolerance, your criticalness, you can automatically know that you do exactly the same with yourself.

If you are in shallow, unsatisfactory relationships which lack depth, gratification, and intimacy, where you reveal yourself only superficially—perhaps only showing your idealized self-image which you think is the only acceptable part of you—again you will have a good gauge of where you are within yourself. You are not even taking a chance because you are unable to accept yourself. Hence you cannot believe that your true, genuine self can ever be accepted, nor can you accept others for where they are in their present state of development. All this excludes mutuality.

The movement of opening up and taking in, the relaxed bliss of streaming into another energy field and accepting the emanation of the other energy field—this bliss is unbearable and appears dangerous if you hate yourself. When you contract after every temporary opening, you can realize that this does not happen because you are evil and do not deserve the bliss, but because you cannot accept the totality of forces and energies as they exist in you now. Therefore you remain locked in the contractions and cannot convert them into expansions.

So, the principle of mutuality must first be applied to the relationship between you and your inner self. Only then can it be extended to your relationship with others. But let me say to you, my friends, from the vantage point of a higher degree of consciousness, that *all the separateness that appears so real in your reality is as much an illusion as the separateness between you and yourself.* It is an artifact that comes into being exclusively because of what is denied. By closing your eyes and your consciousness to the total person you happen to be at this stage, you create apparently two selves: the acceptable and the unacceptable. But in reality there are no two entities: they are both you, whether or not you choose to know this now. But are you really two people? Of course not. The same illusion prevails about all apparently separate entities. Here, too, the separation is an arbitrary, artificial construct of the mind. In reality such a division does not exist. This may not be easy for you to feel at this stage, but the fact remains that human beings live in the overall illusion of separateness which is the cause of pain and struggle. *In reality all is one and every entity is connected with everything else in the universe*—and this is not merely a figure of speech. One consciousness permeates the universe and everything therein. But you can begin to experience this unity only when there is no longer any part of yourself that is excluded, denied, or split off.

Now are there any questions with respect to this topic?

Energy Flow and Mutuality

QUESTION: Can you discuss the aspects of mutuality on the physical, mental, and spiritual levels from the energetic point of view?

ANSWER: Yes. From the energetic point of view the expanding movement is an outgoing and outflowing movement. When two separate human beings open up toward one another in mutuality, able to accept an open flow without contracting, the energy from one interpenetrates the energy field of the other, and vice versa. It is a constant interflow and exchange. It is otherwise with the people who remain separate, who contract, and cannot open up to mutuality. Two such people remain enclosed, each like an island, with little or no energy being exchanged between them. And when exchange of energy is blocked, the great evolutionary plan is delayed.

When a person can open only when there is no chance of mutuality, or when a yes-current must be met with a no-current because mutuality still seems too frightening, one energy flow streams out but reverberates and bounces back, thrown back by the closed energy field of the other. The latter is like a wall that throws off any incoming flow. Thus, the two flows can never become one flow. This phenomenon can easily be observed in everyday life. People either always fall in love when it is not reciprocated, or, for apparently unfathomable reasons, fall out of love when their partner has deep feelings. The same principle exists in ongoing relationships: when one person is open, the other is closed, and vice versa. Only steady development and growth changes this so that both learn to remain open to one another.

On the spiritual and emotional levels, the lowest stage indicates an acute state of fear. *The fear of accepting the self in its present stage is essentially the same fear that wants to run away from true mutuality and bliss.* Since the fear is there, hate must also come into being with all its derivatives.

The mental levels are affected by this process of avoidance when a person seeks ready explanations for what cannot be understood unless the self is accepted for what it is now. The mental activity becomes so busy that it cannot attune to the higher voices within the self, to the deeper truths of the universe. More separation is thus engendered. Mental noise creates more disconnection from the feelings and from the state that first created the condition. Such a person or entity is forced by its own choice to live in a constant state of frustration and unfulfillment. Physically this creates, of course, blocks within the body.

In the second stage, where alternate opening up and contracting occurs, the mental activity of the person is confused. Search and groping cannot yield truthful answers as long as the self is not accepted with its very worst. Mental confusion creates more frustration and anger. The faulty interpretations which are supposed to explain why the person is always missing mutuality only increase frustration, and therefore anger and hate. On the emotional level, longing and disappointment alternate with fulfillment in fantasy. This indicates some degree of opening and flow, although with no real mutuality, but withdrawal and contraction. The latter again includes anger and hate, disappointment and blaming.

When self-acceptance makes mutuality possible and energy is exchanged, the universal movements flow evenly. The healthy alternation of the expanding, contracting, and static principles prevails where individuals find themselves in the eternal rhythm, harmonious with the universe.

Be blessed, my dearest ones. May this lecture again be like a little light shining inside yourself, giving you hope and strength, showing you from yet another side the way, and leading you more strongly toward accepting yourself exactly as you are now. May you not indulge in anything, nor excuse it, but see it for what it is. Accept the imperfection fully, neither embellishing it nor exaggerating it so that you cringe with shame and fear. All these distortions must disappear, for they are pitfalls more disastrous than whatever aspects you hate yourself for. When you find and apply this attitude, you will find your happiness and the truth that unites you with yourself and the universe.

PART II

How to Discover and Overcome the Obstacles to a Fulfilling Relationship

The lectures in this part of the book present in detail the prevalent belief systems, childish expectations, contradictory feelings, and negative patterns that separate us from each other. Why is it so difficult to reach union with another human being?

Though the word "unconscious" is widely used these days, most of us cannot quite grasp what it means to have a vast reservoir of feelings and thoughts whose contents are ordinarily not accessible to us. This would not matter if the inaccessible material did not influence our view of the world, our behavior, our entire life. But it does—with a vengeance. Therefore it is crucial to allow the unconscious material to surface and to learn the secrets of our souls that we have kept hidden even from our own selves.

After describing the inner territory to be explored, the Guide gives precise instructions on how to set about releasing the contents of our unconscious and making it available to examination. Once we know what is there, the inner walls begin to crumble and we can begin the work of self-transformation.

It is as if the Guide took us to the peak of a high mountain to share the view he sees when he looks at human life. He points out the various regions of our souls, those which are healthy and whole and also those which are flawed: the spiritual and emotional quagmires where our unfulfilling relationships have their seeds.

We learn, with amazement, that we rarely know what we really feel, wish, think, or need. Childish, half-formed presumptions, confused feelings, unjustified fears and guilts, self-punishing patterns come to the surface when we are finally willing to find out who we are and how we function as love-partners, as friends. Most of our problems have common roots, because we are all human, which is encouraging to know as we set out to find our specific inner twists and knots.

To heal our own souls is our first task, but this does not mean that we have to wait to engage in a relationship until we are in full harmony within ourselves. Life is to be lived—but with ever greater consciousness. Our relationships will improve accordingly.

There are various ways to coax unconscious, vital material out of hiding. One is through meticulous, openminded, nonjudgmental self-observation. The Guide is unsurpassed in leading the truth-seeker into the labyrinth of his or her infantile world, there to encounter and tame private monsters. We then become ever more ready to open our arms and hearts.

This inner journey is also the way home to the Godself. It can be the greatest adventure of your life: from isolation to fearless loving. Are you ready to embark on it?

                                                                J.S.

Desire for Unhappiness and Fear of Loving

Greetings, my dearest friends. I bring you blessings. Blessed is this hour.

The wish for happiness exists in every living being. However, the concept of happiness varies according to the development of each individual. The infant's idea of happiness is the fulfillment of all its desires instantly and in exactly the way it wants it. A remnant of this childish expectation stays with all human beings for the rest of their lives. This *distorted concept* eventually causes a chain reaction through which another desire comes into existence in the human soul, and that, strange as it may seem, is a *desire for unhappiness.*

The mature concept of happiness in its highest unfoldment could be expressed in these words: "I am independent of outer circumstances, regardless of what they are. I can be happy under any circumstances, because I know that even the disadvantageous or unpleasant events have a purpose. They will teach me something and so bring me nearer to freedom and happiness."

The immature concept of happiness could be stated like this: "I can be happy only if I can have what I want, the way I want it, and when I want it. Otherwise I will be unhappy." Implied in this statement is the demand for absolute approval, admiration, and love by everybody. The moment anyone refuses to meet this requirement, the immature person's world crumbles, as if his or her happiness had been taken away forever. This, of course, is never the intellectual conviction of an adult human being, but emotionally it holds true.

For the undeveloped being, everything feels black or white; there is no in-between. If things happen in accordance with his or her wishes, the world is bright. But if the tiniest little thing goes against the will, then the world looks black.

When the infant is hungry, minutes seem like eternity, not only because the baby lacks a concept of time, but also because it does not know that the period of hunger will soon be over. So the baby cries in absolute despair, fury, and unhappiness. This part of the personality, so freely expressed in infancy, remains hidden in the psyche of the adult human being. There, covered up by rational behavior, it continues to produce similar reactions.

The infant realizes very early that it is impossible to obtain the kind of happiness it wants. It feels dependent on a cruel world, which denies what it thinks it needs, and surely could have if the world were less cruel.

Desire for Omnipotent Rulership

If you think it through logically, you will find that the baby's primitive and distorted concept of happiness actually amounts to a desire for omnipotent rulership, to having a special position in which the surrounding world owes it unquestioned obedience. The child demands from everybody to fulfill what it desires. When this wish cannot be gratified—and it never can—the frustration becomes absolute.

Of course it is impossible for any human being to remember these early emotions, for one has no memory of one's first years. That *these primitive reactions continue to exist without exception in all human beings* is a fact, however. You can discover them in yourself by various methods, for instance by remembering and observing past or present reactions and analyzing them.

First, *discover the infant in you* with its desires and reactions. Focus your attention on this particular aspect of your personality. Until you have experienced the infant in you, you cannot understand certain inner conflicts.

The more the child grows and learns to live in this world, the more it realizes that the omnipotent rulership it wishes for is not only denied but the wish itself is frowned upon. So it learns to hide it until the desire fades into oblivion. The repression brings about two basic reactions. One is: "Perhaps, if I become perfect, as the world around me asks me to be, I will get so much approval that through it I can attain my goal." Striving for such perfection then begins. Needless to say, my friends, that though we are all in agreement that all beings should strive for perfection, this kind of striving is wrong. It is wrong because of the motive: the person does not strive for perfection in order to love better and give more, but for the selfish end to reach, through immediate perfection, the omnipotent rulership it desires. That is, of course, utterly impossible.

Thus, the frustration becomes a double one: the first objective—omnipotent rulership in order to be happy—is not realized; neither is the second desire fulfilled, that of attaining perfection in order to obtain the first desire. This failure, in turn, causes acute feelings of inadequacy and inferiority, of regret and guilt. For the child does not know yet that no one is capable of attaining such perfection. It thinks itself unique in having failed and has to hide this shameful fact. Even the adult who consciously knows better will, unconsciously, still argue: "If I could be perfect, I would have what I want. Since I am not perfect, I am worth nothing."

Refusal of Self-Responsibility

At the same time, there is yet another reaction. One cannot, and does not want to assume the entire blame for one's failure, and therefore one blames one's surroundings. The inward argument goes as follows: "If they allowed me to be happy my way, by loving and approving of me completely and doing what I wish, then I could be perfect. The obstacle that now stands in the way of my getting what I want would be removed. Therefore, it is 'their' fault. My failures are due only to their constant denying of my wishes." So a particular two-way vicious circle comes into existence, which goes like this in one direction: "I need to be perfect in order to be loved and to be happy," and in the other direction: "If I could have the position of rulership I need in order to be happy, then it would not be difficult for me to be perfect." Neither goal is possible to reach. For this the person blames the world on the one hand, and the self on the other.

The wrong concept of happiness is inevitably linked with a wrong concept of love, because, just as with happiness, the infant in you believes that the proof of love is that your every wish is fulfilled. Therefore, in order to feel loved, you need "slaves" who surrender to your every desire: "If I am loved, I must be paid homage; then I possess a subject." If you believe that this is so—as the infant inside every human being does—it follows that you must be afraid of loving, for when *you* love, *you* must become the slave. If you very honestly observe your reactions, you will find such feelings in you, although you may never have had the courage to acknowledge them. Try to remember and recognize those occasions when you wanted to have a subject to serve you instead of an object to love.

As you recognize your own unconscious childish distortion about love, you will be able to sense the childish demands of the other person. Also, when you discover and experience the existence of the unfair demands of the child in you, you can reason with it. Then you are bound to realize that love does not mean giving up dignity, self-government, or freedom, and therefore you will not fear it. Now you prohibit your capacity to love due to the confused notion that true love equals submissiveness, and you distrust others because you have an inordinate demand for being loved and served.

When you are immature, you do not accept reality, since reality is not always perfect or pleasant: every wish of yours is not fulfilled every time. Only as you grow and learn to face and accept whatever exists in your everyday life and emotions will you lose your fear of loving. As you grow in maturity, you will realize that you can hope to reach the final fulfillment of love only by starting on the lower steps of the ladder. Perhaps one of these is the ability of *allowing other people to feel about you as they wish.* If you can give this "inner permission" genuinely, you will get to the point where you can truly like and respect others, even if they don't submit to your will all the way. In such a gradual process of growth and maturing, you will eventually overcome the conflict in which your soul yearns to experience great, all-encompassing love, while at the same time hiding from it in fear.

The Right Concept of Love

For this to happen, you need to know the right concept of love. *Love is the greatest power in the universe.* Every spiritual teaching or philosophy, every religion, even modern psychology proclaims this truth. With it you are mighty, you are strong, you are safe. Without it you are poor, separate, in seclusion and fear. The right concept of love includes the kind of loving where you love regardless of whether or not the other person loves you. Such love is unconditional. But if you are not that far, it is useless trying to force yourself. The compulsion and the inability to follow through would only increase your feelings of failure and guilt. This, in turn, would lead to a self-destructive tendency. Moreover, the desire for ideal, unselfish love can easily be distorted by an *unhealthy desire to suffer.* So, if momentarily you are not loved and find it impossible to love, simply recognize it without guilt. That is the first step toward transformation.

The Desire for Unhappiness

Now how does all this lead to the desire for unhappiness? As I said, the human personality finds it increasingly impossible to find happiness according to these wrong concepts formed in childhood. Instead of finding the right way by replacing the wrong concepts with the right ones, *you are trying to force life into the wrong concepts.* When this proves impossible, another way out is sought, which seems to be a solution but proves even more damaging in the long run. The inner argument goes on in the unconscious: "Since happiness is denied me and unhappiness is inevitable and inflicted on me against my will, I may just as well make the best of it and turn a liability into an asset. Since I cannot avoid unhappiness, I may just as well enjoy it. Furthermore, I want to alleviate the humiliation of feeling a helpless prey to this unhappiness that is inflicted upon me against my will. If I call forth the unhappiness myself, I am not quite so helpless."

Superficially, this may appear to be a smart solution, but of course it never is. Although certain aspects of unhappiness *can* be enjoyed in an unhealthy way, there are bound to be other aspects that are extremely painful and *cannot* be enjoyed at all. But of this you are ignorant to begin with; you did not bargain for it, and when it happens, you fail to see the connection with the process described here. Since the entire process is unconscious anyway, the unenjoyable aspects of unhappiness are never connected with the notion that the unhappiness was self-produced. Only by tracing these emotions and reactions in the course of your self-work will you find the patterns of how you go on and on in subtle, hidden ways, *provoking people* and bringing about certain situations, so that *you can collect unhappy incidents, injustices, injuries, wrongs, and hurts.* Once you find out how you have provoked all this, you will also be able to find out what you *enjoy* about it in a certain way—no matter how much you loathe some aspects of it in your conscious mind. You might enjoy, for instance, the provocation itself or the self-pity that ensues. All this seldom happens in a very obvious way, although sometimes it is quite noticeable to others, but not to you. Most of the time it happens so subtly that it completely escapes your attention—unless *you truly wish to notice it.*

This wrong way out also uses the following childish inner argument: "Since only black and white exist, and white is denied me, let me enjoy the all-black." This inner process sets the entire chain reaction into renewed momentum. Because the desire for unhappiness is unconscious, the injuries collected in the process of provoking the unhappiness make you feel even more inadequate, the world even more cruel and unfair.

It is often said that self-destructiveness, that is, the desire for unhappiness, is the result of deep-rooted guilt feelings. This is only partly true. It is much rather the other way around. *The real guilt and shame come from provoking unhappiness and collecting miseries. That is the mother of all guilts.*

When you are ready to face all this within yourself, truly experiencing these feelings, your life will gradually begin to change in many ways. By recognizing again and again the ways in which you call forth unhappiness, you will cease to do so. You will realize that *there is no longer any need for it.* When you achieve a more mature outlook on life, you will cease to desire being a ruler. To the degree that you learn to give up this false desire voluntarily, you will give up provoking unhappiness and misery. Then one of the obstacles to having a fulfilling relationship, in which you can feel happy as well as loving and loved, will be removed.

Be blessed, all of you who hear or read my words. May divine light and strength, truth and love flow through you and lighten your burdens. Be in peace, be in God.

CHAPTER 7

*The Valid Desire
to Be Loved*

Greetings, my dearest friends. Blessings for each one of you. Blessed is this hour. May you each find guidance where you most need it.

On the path of self-search one learns not only to deal better with difficulties, but also with happy times. The person who is still in darkness and ignorance about the facts of human existence and the significance of life can handle the good happenings no better than the adverse ones. Both need wisdom, maturity, and the spiritual knowledge that gives the true incentive for self-knowledge, so that your search can be conducted constructively.

The desire to be loved exists in every human soul. This desire in itself is not only legitimate and healthy, but it is also in its own way creative, or it leads to becoming creative. Lack of love can lead to a paralysis of the soul's creative forces. To fulfill the soul's longing to be loved, people often choose a wrong way, partly because the longing is unconscious. Until the longing can be examined in the light of reason and reality, it functions abortively and therefore creates frustrations. Why then is this desire so often unconscious? Let us first examine the reason.

The child's desire for love is limitless, but he or she is made to feel that such a desire for exclusive and limitless love is wrong; therefore it feels guilty about it. It is true that wishing for exclusive and limitless love is unrealistic and immature. But because the wish remains unfulfilled, the child comes to the wrong conclusion that the desire for love in itself is wrong. The right conclusion would be: "The type of love I wanted so far cannot be mine. But I do have a right to be loved. This can happen provided that I, on my part, learn to love in the right and mature way."

Shame of the Longing

The first misunderstanding, then, is that the longing to be loved is something to be ashamed of. The longing is buried, and because it is buried, many unhappy consequences come into being.

You may think, "With me, this longing is not buried at all. I am completely aware of it." Yes, you may indeed be aware of the longing—to a degree. But even so you remain only partly conscious of the inner sadness, the unfulfilled longing, and of the struggle within to cover up the sadness and to fight for a *substitute* for the love you lack. The fight wears you out, and it causes reactions that defeat the very end you wish to achieve. Each one of you, in your own way, needs to see how and where you can link up your own conflicts with this universal struggle.

In spite of your shame about your yearning for love and your subsequent suppression of it, you cannot silence this clamoring voice completely. The voice is there, but it can only express itself in a devious way, and this deviousness is responsible for your not getting the love you yearn for. But you do not yet know that. You believe deep down, "It is wrong for me to seek to be loved. I have no right to be loved, I am not worthy of it. That is why I do not get it." But the inner voice that can never be stilled goes on fighting in its own erroneous way, with the very attitude that is bound to make you less lovable. If you were to give up the wrong way of searching, you would realize that the real you can be loved and will be loved. The vicious circle would then be broken.

Substitution of Approval for Love

Now, what is this wrong way? You substitute for your desire to be loved the desire to be approved of, to shine, to be better than others, to impress people, to be important. Somehow this seems less shameful. Thus you are going through life constantly proving yourself. The substitution may assume various other forms. People have to agree with you, to follow in your footsteps, or you have to prove to them that you agree with them, that you conform with public opinion or the opinion of certain people, or what you think their opinion is—and that is not always the same. All these and many others are mere substitutes for your longing to be loved.

The frequent tendency to conform, to be the "obedient child," is part of this conflict. Different tendencies can come to the fore with different kinds of people. Within yourself you are unaware of the original desire, often even unaware of the substitute desire—the fight of proving yourself to others.

The compulsion to prove something exists in everyone, only the degree varies. As long as you do not understand the nature of this compulsion—after you have verified its existence in you—you cannot see any solution and you will be unable to give up the compulsive fight. But if you will search in the right direction, you will not only *know* in your intellect that the sadness of your unfulfillment exists, but you will also *feel* it—and that is good. You will then realize that your fight for approval, to prove something or other, makes you self-centered, proud, arrogant, superior—or unhealthily submissive which is bound to make you resentful. The struggle contributes strongly to the adverse result of people not loving you, whereas you *could* be loved if you were free of the entire layer that still desires a substitution instead of the real thing. If you have allowed yourself to feel the original longing, not being afraid of the supposed "humiliation" and "weakness" this desire implies, nor being afraid of feeling simple sadness that will never have an unhealthy effect on your soul, you will contribute greatly toward your fulfillment. You will realize that it is not you who are not good enough to be loved, but that the artificial mask you laboriously constructed is what is unacceptable. You will then not wallow in damaging self-pity, but will grow sufficiently to shed those tendencies that prevent you from receiving what you should.

Moreover, you will realize that your fight is completely useless. Nothing that is inauthentic can ever bring success. And a superimposed layer, covering an original wish, is never genuine. Even if you succeed temporarily in getting what you fight for—admiration, approval, whatever it may be—it will leave you unsatisfied and with a bitter taste. You are bound to be disappointed, for you cannot ever get it to the degree you reach for, it cannot be permanent and coming from as many fellow-humans as you wish and, above all, because it is not what you really desire. Your frustration and unhappiness always has this conflict at the roots.

You fight as though your life is at stake—inwardly you do. You need to recognize this conflict before you can find the original desire to be loved and the sadness that you are not loved as you could be. Think how very frequently it happens that your emotions react disproportionately when someone disagrees with you. But if you are deeply convinced that someone loves you with all his heart and kindness, manifesting it with warmth and tenderness, the disagreement does not matter. Each one of you will be able to recall such instances. That should serve as a proof that my words also apply to you.

After you recognize these emotions in yourself, you will understand that you are fighting for something you do not really want and that you can never get commensurately to the desperate intensity of your struggle. Find specifically how this fight to prove something, or yourself, in one way or another, brings out the worst in you. What exactly is that? The recognition will be less painful and much more liberating than you think. For you will then understand the reason why you were not loved as much as you wished and will see that it was not because you are who you are, and cannot help it. This will encourage and strengthen you.

As your fight for proving yourself diminishes, you prepare the way for real, mature love. Your maturing mind will make you understand that the only kind of love that *is* love is the kind that is given to you freely. First you will begin *allowing other people to not love you if they do not choose to.* That may make you sad, but it will never make you tense, or compulsive, or intense. This sadness will be free of self-pity and it will not be a real hardship for you. Therefore it will not make you unpleasant.

Forcing Others to Love You

Inwardly, you constantly want to force others to love you. The outer cover is the approval, but in the last analysis you want to force people to love you, and forced love is no love. The child in you does not see that. But as you recognize these currents, you will detect the current within yourself that says quite clearly, "you *must* love me." Weaker persons with unhealthy motives of their own may appear to give in temporarily and obey your command. But such response can only leave you empty and disappointed, since it is not what you are really striving for and what cannot be had as long as the forcing current is not dissolved. For the strong and mature soul cannot be coerced into submission. It functions only in freedom. Moreover, you will never really respect the person who obeys this command. You will respect only the person who loves you freely. You can have the chance of experiencing this free gift only if you don't force it, however. *You can never experience the free gift of love as long as the forcing current operates undetected by your consciousness.* Thus you first have to let people free by permitting them not to love you, if they so choose. That does not mean you have to be happy about it, but face the sadness and it will not harm you. The reward will be tremendous if someone then offers you his or her love freely. You will then understand that *you* had been denying yourself the chance of receiving the only true and valuable love that exists.

Please, my friends, do not misunderstand. When I say you force others to love you, I do not refer to any conscious action on your part. I am speaking of your emotions. If you understand what underlies your emotional reactions to people, you will see that it amounts to that.

Giving Freedom

You will learn how to make the generous gesture of giving freedom to others not only to be wrong, or to disagree with you, or to have weaknesses which you may not approve of, but also not to love you. If you are conscious of your original desire, and then of your frustration, and then of what you do in your frustration, and then of the forcing current in you, you will clearly see that only by these emotional attitudes in your unconscious do you forfeit the free gift of real love— and not because you are not good enough. Then you are on the road upward.

Let us further examine another aspect of the inner *universal* process I have just described. You long for being loved while you are more or less unable to give love, at least to the degree that you desire it for yourself. Your love functions at best only if people do right by you. Hence, you request something of others that you are inwardly unwilling to give them. You request unconditional love. You expect to be so well understood that people love you in spite of your shortcomings and various weaknesses. You do not realize that with these very weaknesses you hurt and disappoint them inadvertently just as often as others inadvertently hurt and disappoint you due to *their* weaknesses. *You* want to be understood and loved in spite of them. But you are not willing to do the same if other people's weaknesses affect you negatively. This request—unspoken and unconscious—is unfair; it amounts to pride, for you claim an extra position that you are not willing to concede to others. This position is highly subjective and therefore unrealistic. Such attitudes manifest and affect the other person more strongly than you can possibly realize now. It is easy to see that their effect will not be in your favor.

Thus, it is necessary that you learn to love, for only then will this affect others in a way that they will have to give you love. In learning how to love, the first step is to eliminate your subjectivity. *Love is objectivity* among many other things. Subjectivity is self-centered, and love and self-centeredness cannot exist side by side. You all know that love cannot be forced; it will grow organically as you remove the obstacles. The inherent self-concern and subjectivity is one of the greatest blocks to your giving and receiving love.

The Willingness to Love

No human being is ever completely capable of *real* love and *real* objectivity. But there are degrees. To the degree you observe your lack of objectivity, you approach objectivity and, thereby, the capacity to love.

Your capacity to love increases steadily as your willingness to love increases. The willingness to love, in turn, will grow proportionately as you no longer feel terrified of not being loved in return, or not in exactly the way or at the speed you would want it. Recognize your fright of every little hurt and disappointment. As you focus your inner view in that direction, you will surely come to see your terror as a total illusion, as your overgrown imagination. Because of it, you are *unwilling* to love. Therefore your capacity to love is constantly diminished and paralyzed. When you have gained the capacity to have an objective and detached view, you cannot possibly allow the unhealthy instincts of others to hurt you. You will no longer have the misconception that a masochistic tendency is proof of love. You will be rid of the illusion that every slight, hurt, or disappointment is a tragedy against which you have to guard yourself.

To recapitulate: The solution of the problem of knowing how to give and receive love demands that you recognize 1) your substitute emotions which find gratification through the subtle current of forcing others to love you; 2) your subjective outlook, hidden in your emotional reactions, that makes you unable to give love; 3) your world of illusion wherein you are in terror of being rejected; 4) the effect all this has on your personality and on your surroundings.

Full recognition of these elements takes time, perseverance and very effective will on your part to face *anything* that is within yourself, without reservation. As the truth of these words becomes alive in you, you are bound to gradually change these elements and attitudes, slowly but surely. With this willingness, your capacity to love will increase. You will show discrimination in the kind of love you are willing to give others, and you will not be disturbed by the realization that not all people love you according to the demands of the child in you. When some people do not love you, or even disapprove of you, this will no longer be the tragedy which it now is when your emotions register such incidents.

As you grow and mature, not being loved, or being disapproved of, will not upset you. And as it does not upset you, it will not bring out the worst in you. You will take life's disappointments with a certain equanimity. You will become capable of having sympathy for, and an objective nondistorted view of, those who anger you. This will be your reality deep down in your emotions, not superficially and in an artificially manufactured fashion.

May these words be the beginning of a new phase on a deeper level for each one of you. Pray for deeper understanding of the words I gave you tonight. Be blessed in the name of the Most Holy. Go in peace and in joy on your path of liberation. Move toward maturity and reality in a joyful and patient spirit. Many will be the fruits of this work for all of those who do not let up. Be blessed, be in peace, be in God.

Objectivity and Subjectivity in Relationship

Greetings, my dearest friends. I bring you very special blessings tonight. The strong forces of love coming to you touch all spheres. Whoever is open and in a state of quiet harmony can receive this force that is a blessing for your body, your soul, and your spirit.

I have touched on the topic of objectivity and subjectivity occasionally. Now I will discuss it in greater detail, for objectivity is essential for a free and harmonious human being and for a harmonious relationship. The more unpurified and disharmonious you are, the less objective you will be. Objectivity means truth. Subjectivity means colored truth, half-truth at best, complete untruth in many cases. Contrary to a conscious lie, subjectivity results in unconscious or unintended untruth. All this emanates from the emotional level of a person's being.

At first, as you do the purification work, you will find the untruth that exists in the depths of your soul. After the untruth is ousted, you will be able to plant truth within yourself. Only a path of stringent self-search will make such discoveries and the ensuing change possible. This lecture will give you an additional angle from which to look at your relationships in general and at yourself in particular. It will help you to advance a step further.

Let us first take the common phenomenon that what you see as a grave fault in others, you often do not see in yourself. It makes no difference whether the fault is exactly the same or whether it has a slightly different and modified form. Your objection to the faults you observe in others—especially your partner—may even be correct. Yet you are in half-truth when you judge the other while you fail to see how you also deviate from what is right and good in a similar way. Furthermore, the fault of the other may coexist with good qualities you yourself do not possess. Thus your judgment is colored, for you concentrate your objection on one sore point, while you leave out of sight many facets that would complete the picture.

Concentrating on the Other's Faults

So, my dear friends, whenever you judge someone, whenever you resent his or her faults, please ask yourself: "Don't I, perhaps in a different way, have a similar fault? And doesn't the person whom I judge so harshly have some good qualities that I lack?" Then think of the good qualities the other possesses and you lack. Remember also to ask yourself whether you do not have faults that the person you judge and resent does not have. This consideration will help you to assess your anger at other people's—especially your partner's—faults more objectively. And *if by chance the outcome of this evaluation turns out to be that your faults are really so much less and your good qualities so much superior to the other's, that is all the more reason to cultivate your tolerance and understanding.* If you did so, you would indeed be in a higher state of development, which means, above all, the obligation to be understanding and forgiving. If you lack that ability, all your superior qualities mean nothing! But if you make serious endeavors in that direction, your Godself will help you to be more objective. You will thus definitely have more peace, and that which now bothers you so very much will cease to upset you.

Whenever you are upset about another person's faults, there must be something in you that is not right either. You know this, friends, but you forget it again and again when opportunities come up to examine yourself. *You should not be concerned with the fact that the other person may be so obviously in the wrong, so much more wrong than you are.* Try to find the little grain of imperfection in yourself instead of concentrating on the mountain in the other. For it is your own unhealthy grain of untruth that robs you of peace and never the mountain of wrong in the other person!

Two Defensive Measures: Severity and Idealization

There is another form of extreme subjectivity that comes from the same root although it manifests in a very different way. Many human beings are very severe with those who make them feel unloved and criticized, or at least insecure. Their severity is a defense. If you rest secure in your value, you will not feel insecure and you will therefore develop a natural tolerance. But most of you are still so insecure that you resort to defective defensive measures. This behavior falls into the same category as blindly idealizing the person in whose love you feel secure. In such cases you do not see the very trends you most strenuously object to in someone else. That is dangerous too, my dear ones, expecially because this tendency lends itself extremely well to deceiving yourself into believing that your idealization is love and tolerance. You try to convince yourself that you are tolerant and good when you close your eyes to the faults of those you love because they love you. No, my friends, that is not true loving. True love can see reality. If you are ready to love in the most vital and mature way, you will not try to close your eyes to the faults of the loved one, but will do the opposite.

If you do close your eyes persistently, it is for two reasons. One is pride: the one you have chosen as your loved one and the one who has chosen you as the loved one must not have faults which you do not consider acceptable. Oh, you may admit to some faults in the other, as you admit to some faults in yourself, knowing that no human being exists without weaknesses. But you continue to ignore many trends, half-consciously thinking that this attitude proves your love and tolerance, but it is done really out of pride. The second reason is that *deep down in your heart you are so insecure about your own ability to love that you need an idealized version of the loved person.* Your love is not true love if you are compelled to see this person in an idealized form. No, it is a weakness and often a bondage.

Real love is freedom, dear friends. It can stand the test of truth as it prevails in the other person at this moment of his or her development. When you reach that stage, you will be able to see the one who is dear to your heart as he or she really is and not the way you want to. As long as you close your eyes to the real picture of the other, you are not capable of love. Indeed, you are so aware of your incapacity, though on a rather superficial, subconscious level, that you keep busily closing your eyes, afraid that if you saw the truth, you could not go on loving. Pride, and your present inability to truly love, make you go from one extreme to the other. Either you refuse to see the person who is close and dear to you as he or she truly is, or else you judge too harshly, even though the criticism in itself may be justified. The isolated fact that you object to may be valid, but not your evaluation of the whole person who has so many facets that you have no way of knowing.

How to Avoid a Crisis of Awakening

When you persist in being blind to the faults of your loved ones, a crisis, a shake-up, and a painful awakening that will hurt deeply is often unavoidable. Actually, it is not the other person who will then have disappointed and hurt you, but your own past *deliberate* blindness. In such a crisis, this blindness is what deep down you resent most of all. Avoid such a crisis, my dear ones. If you learn to see and love other people as they really are, you can do so.

I would like to give the following advice to you, my friends: Think of the people you love most in the world, and then make a list of their good qualities and of their faults, just as you are currently doing for yourself. Then ask some mutual friends: "Please tell me, what do you think? Am I right? I would appreciate your opinion about these persons' qualities and faults, whether or not you see them as I do, so that I can check out whether I am objective or not. I ask this for the purpose of my development." Then compare how you and how others, who are perhaps more detached and objective than you, see the same people.

Observe your reactions on hearing of faults you either could not or would not conceive of in those whom you idealize. When you become angry and hurt inside, this should be a sign that you are not objective, that you fear the truth, most probably because of the two reasons already stated: pride, and your inability to love people as they really are. Otherwise you would remain calm, even if your beloved is accused of a fault he or she does not possess. Considering the faults of their beloveds might be very healthy for some of my friends. You will learn to evaluate the people you love, and your love will mature and grow in stature. *Thus you will grow out of the immature state in which you love like a frightened child who cannot see the truth.*

Discover a Child's Mentality in Yourself

I have spoken about the childish mentality that continues to exist in your unconscious misconceptions. The child knows only extremes: good or bad, perfection or imperfection, omnipotence that promises security, or utter weakness that it must avoid. The child can accept only the first of these alternatives. When it discovers that an adored parent has faults and is not omnipotent, it either turns away from the parent and begins to hate and resent, feels let down and disappointed, or else it hides the discovery in the unconscious, feeling guilty about having found something unworthy in the parent. These reactions continue to live in the soul of the adult and color his or her reactions and behavior patterns throughout life, or as long as they have not been reviewed and reevaluated in the light of mature judgment and reality. When you look at your present relationships from this point of view, the process will be painful at first, but not half as bad as your unconscious resistance would want to make you believe. Do not heed it. Go on in your search for truth. I can promise that you will evolve a much happier, freer and securer person.

Put Your Vision Into Focus

I beg you not to say offhand that you do see the faults of your loved ones, especially your partner. Yes, you may see some of their faults, but perhaps only those you can tolerate; the others you may not allow yourself to see. Thus you have no conception of his or her entire personality. You see a picture that is just as distorted as when you are too severe and intolerant. The picture is out of focus in both instances; both are mirrors that do not reflect reality. Each mirror distorts in a different way. You are so scared to approach the truth because the emotion of the child for whom seeing an unpleasant truth in the beloved person is unbearable still lives within you, and this recognition forces you to withdraw your love. But that is not the truth at all. *If you approach this particular search with the knowledge that your love, instead of weakening must grow and mature, you can overcome your resistance to finding out the reality.*

You must know which one of the two exremes of subjectivity is more important for you to tackle first. Both alternatives will apply to all of you, but one of them always stands in the foreground. Start by concentrating on that one.

Objectivity needs courage too, my friends. Many of you are still too weak to see the truth in others, as well as in yourselves. *Mature love means to love others in spite of their faults*, knowing them, seeing them, not closing one's eyes to them, and then to build on the good that is already there. Immature love means to view the other person in terms of either/or, though you may have moderated this attitude somewhat as your intellect has matured. You may admit to certain faults which do not violate your personal standards and concepts. *To judge people harshly, as though all human beings were on the same level of development, is equally immature.* The other person may not even be less developed than you; he or she may simply be developed in another respect. Therefore you cannot compare or judge. *Simply see.* If you cannot see without anger, you need to realize that this reaction stems from the same origin as the other extreme, namely, that you cannot accept imperfection and are thus emotionally still a child. See your still existing inability to love. Pray to give up your illusions, your vanity, your pride. Upon this truth you can then erect true love.

My dear, dear friends, angels of God are here tonight to bless you. This blessing extends also to all who are absent, to all who follow these teachings. Continue on this path, my dear ones, and you will gain the strength of love and understanding that can be yours only when you go into the depths of your being to face yourself in truth. Be in peace, be in God.

CHAPTER 9

Compulsion to Re-create and Overcome Childhood Hurts

Greetings, my dearest friends. God bless all of you. May the divine blessings extended to every one of you help you assimilate the words I speak tonight, so that this will be a fruitful occasion for you.

The Lack of Mature Love

Because children so seldom receive sufficient mature love and warmth, they continue to hunger for it throughout their lives unless this lack and hurt is recognized and properly dealt with. If not, *as adults they will go through life unconsciously crying out for what they missed in childhood.* This will make them incapable of loving maturely. You can see how this condition continues from generation to generation.

The remedy cannot be found by wishing that things were different and that people would learn to practice mature love. The remedy lies solely in you. True, if you had received such love from your parents, you would be without this problem of which you are not really and fully aware. But this lack of receiving mature love need trouble neither you nor your life if you become aware of it, see it, and rearrange your former unconscious wishes, regrets, thoughts and concepts by aligning them to the reality of each situation. As a consequence, you will not only become a happier person, but you will also be able to extend mature love to others—to your children, if you have any, or to other people in your environment—so that a benign chain reaction can start. Such realistic self-correction is very contrary to your present inner behavior which we shall now consider.

All people, including even those few who have started to explore their own unconscious mind and emotions, habitually overlook the strong link between the child's longing and unfulfillment and the adult's present difficulties and problems, because only very few people experience personally—and not just recognize in theory—how strong this link is. Full awareness of it is essential.

There may be isolated, exceptional cases where one parent offers a sufficient degree of mature love. Even if one parent has it to some measure, very likely the other does not. Since mature love on this earth is only present to a degree, the child will suffer from the shortcomings of even a loving parent.

More often, however, both parents are emotionally imma-ture and cannot give the love the child craves, or give it only in insufficient measure. During childhood, this need is rarely conscious. Children have no way of putting their needs into thoughts. They cannot compare what they have with what others have. They do not know that something else might exist. They believe this is the way it should be. Or, in extreme cases, they feel especially isolated, believing their lot is like no one else's. Both attitudes deviate from the truth. In both cases the real emotion is not conscious and therefore cannot be properly evaluated and come to terms with. Thus, children grow up never quite understanding why they are unhappy, nor even that they are unhappy. Many of you look back on childhood convinced that you had all the love you wanted just because you actually did have some love.

There are a number of parents who give great demonstra-tions of love. They may overindulge their children. Such spoiling and pampering may be an overcompensation and a sort of apology for a deeply suspected inability to love maturely. Children feel the truth very acutely. They may not consciously think about it, but inwardly children keenly feel the difference between mature, genuine love and the immature, over-demonstrative variety offered instead.

Proper guidance and security are the parents' responsibility and call for authority on their part. There are parents who never dare to punish or exert a healthy authority. This failing is due to guilt because real, giving, warming, comforting love is absent in their own immature personalities. Other parents may be too severe, too strict. They thereby exert a domineering authority by bullying the child and not allowing its individuality to unfold. Both types fall short as parents, and their wrong attitudes, absorbed by the child, will cause hurt and unfulfillment.

In children of the strict parents, the resentment and rebellion will be open, and therefore more easily traced. In the other case, the rebellion is just as strong, but hidden, and therefore infinitely harder to trace. If you had a parent who smothered you with affection or pseudo-affection, yet lacked in genuine warmth, or if you had a parent who conscientiously did everything right but was also lacking in real warmth, unconsciously you knew it as a child and you resented it. Consciously you may not have been aware of it at all, because, when a child, you really could not put your finger on what was lacking. You were outwardly given everything you wanted and needed. How could you draw the subtle, fine borderline distinction between real affection and pseudo-affection with your child's intellect? The fact that something bothered you without your being able to explain it rationally made you feel guilty and uncomfortable. You therefore pushed it out of sight as far as possible.

As long as the hurt, disappointment, and unfulfilled needs of your early years remain unconscious, you cannot come to terms with them. No matter how much you may love your parents, an unconscious resentment exists in you, which prevents you from forgiving them for the hurt. You can only forgive and let go if you recognize your deeply hidden hurt and resentment. As an adult human being you will see that your parents, too, are just human beings. They were not as faultless and perfect as the child had thought and hoped them to be, yet they are not to be rejected now because they had their own conflicts and immaturities. The light of conscious reasoning has to be applied to these very emotions you never allowed yourself to be aware of fully.

Attempts to Remedy the Childhood Hurt in Adulthood

As long as you are unaware of the conflict between your longing for a perfect love from your parents and your resentment against them, you are bound to try remedying the situation in your later years. This striving may manifest in various aspects of your life. You run constantly into problems and repeated patterns which have their origin in your attempt to *reproduce the childhood situation so as to correct it.* This unconscious compulsion is a very strong factor, but is so deeply hidden from your conscious understanding!

The most frequent way of attempting to remedy the situation is in your *choice of love partners. Unconsciously you will know how to choose in the partner aspects of the parent who has particularly fallen short in affection and love that is real and genuine.* But you also seek in your partner aspects of the other parent who has come closer to meeting your demands. Important as it is to find both parents represented in your partners, it is even more important and more difficult to find those aspects which represent the parent who has particularly disappointed and hurt you, the one more resented or despised and for whom you had little or no love. So you seek the parents again—in a subtle way that is not always easy to detect, in your marital partners, in your friendships, or in other human relationships. Subconsciously, the following reactions take place in you: The child in you cannot let go of the past, cannot come to terms with it, cannot forgive, cannot understand and accept, and therefore this very child in you always creates similar conditions, trying to win out in the end in order to finally master the situation instead of succumbing to it. Losing out means being crushed—this must be avoided at all costs. The costs are high indeed, for the entire strategy is unfeasible. What the child in you sets out to accomplish cannot ever come to realization.

The Detrimental Effect of this Strategy on Relationships

This entire procedure is utterly destructive. In the first place, it is an illusion that you were defeated. Therefore, it is an illusion that you can now be victorious. Moreover, it is an illusion that the lack of love, sad as that may have been when you were a child, is indeed the tragedy that you subconsciously still feel it to be. The only tragedy lies in the fact that you obstruct your future happiness by continuing to reproduce the situation and then attempting to master it. My friends, this process is a deeply unconscious one. Of course, nothing is further from your mind as you focus on your conscious aims and wishes. It will take a great deal of digging to uncover the emotions that lead you again and again into situations where your secret aim is to remedy childhood woes.

In trying to reproduce the childhood situation, you unconsciously choose a partner with aspects similar to those of the parent. Yet it is these very aspects which will make it as impossible to receive the mature love you rightfully long for now as it was then. Blindly, you believe that by willing it more strongly and more forcefully, the parent-partner will now yield, whereas in reality love cannot come that way. *Only when you are free of this ever continuing repetition will you no longer cry to be loved by the parent. Instead, you will look for a partner or for other human relationships with the aim of finding the maturity you really need and want.* In not demanding to be loved as a child, you will be equally willing to love. However, the child in you finds this impossible, no matter how much you may otherwise be capable of it through development and progress. This hidden conflict eclipses your otherwise growing soul.

If you already have a partner, the uncovering of this conflict may show you how he or she is similar to your parents in certain immature aspects. But since you now know that there is hardly a really mature person, these immaturities in your partner will no longer be the tragedy they were while you constantly sought to find your parent or parents again, which of course could never come to pass. With your existing immaturity and incapacity, you may nevertheless build a more mature relationship, free of the childish compulsion to re-create and correct the past.

You have no idea how preoccupied your unconscious is with the process of reenacting the play, so to speak, only hoping that "this time it will be different." And it never is! As time goes on, each disappointment weighs heavier and your soul becomes more and more discouraged.

For those of my friends who have not yet reached certain depths of their unexplored unconscious, this may sound quite preposterous and contrived. However, those of you who have come to see the power of your hidden trends, compulsions, and images will not only readily believe it, but will soon experience the truth of these words in their own personal lives. You already know from other findings how potent are the workings of your unconscious mind, how shrewdly it goes about its destructive and illogical ways.

Reexperiencing the Childhood Hurt

If you learn to look at your problems and unfulfillment from this point of view and follow the usual process of allowing your emotions to come to the fore, you will gain much further insight. But it will be necessary, my friends, to reexperience the longing and the hurt of the crying child you were once, even though you were also a happy one. Your happiness may have been valid and without self-deception at all. For it is possible to be both happy and unhappy. You may now be perfectly aware of the happy aspects of your childhood, but that which hurt deeply and that certain something you greatly longed for—you did not even quite know what—you were not aware of. You took the situation for granted. You did not know what was missing or even that there was anything missing. This basic unhappiness has to come to awareness now, if you really want to proceed in inner growth. You have to reexperience the acute pain you once suffered but pushed out of sight. Now you have to look at this pain conscious of the understanding you have gained. Only by doing this will you grasp the reality value of your current problems and see them in their true light.

Now, *how can you manage to reexperience the hurts of so long ago?* There is only one way, my friends. Take a current problem. Strip it of all the superimposed layers of your reactions. The first and most handy layer is that of rationalization, that of "proving" that others, or situations, are at fault, not your innermost conflicts which make you adopt the wrong attitude to the actual problem that confronts you. The next layer might be anger, resentment, anxiety, frustration. Behind all these reactions you will find the hurt of not being loved. When you experience the hurt of not being loved in your current dilemma, it will serve to reawaken the childhood hurt. While you face the present hurt, think back and try to reconsider the situation with your parents: what they gave you, how you really felt about them. You will become aware that in many ways you lacked a certain something you never clearly saw before—you did not want to see it. You will find that this must have hurt you when you were a child, but you may have forgotten the hurt on a conscious level. Yet it is not forgotten at all. The hurt of your current problem is the very same hurt. Now, reevaluate your present hurt, comparing it with the childhood hurt. At last you will clearly see how it is one and the same. No matter how true and understandable your present pain is, it is nevertheless the same childhood pain. A little later you will come to see how you contributed to bringing about the present pain because of your desire to correct the childhood hurt. But at first you only have to feel the similarity of the pain. However, this requires considerable effort, for there are many overlaying emotions that cover the present pain as well as the past one. Before you have succeeded in crystallizing the pain you are experiencing, you cannot understand anything further in this respect.

Once you can synchronize these two pains and realize that they are one and the same, the next step is much easier. Then, by perceiving the repetitious pattern in your various difficulties, you will learn to recognize the similarities between your parents and the people who have caused you hurt or are causing you pain now. Experiencing these similarities emotionally will carry you further on the particular road toward dissolving this basic conflict. Mere intellectual evaluation will not yield any benefit. To be fruitful and bring real results, the process of giving up the recreation must go beyond mere intellectual knowledge. You have to allow yourself to feel the pain of certain unfulfillments now and also the pain of the unfulfillment of your childhood, then compare the two until, like two separate picture slides, they gradually move into focus and become one. *Experiencing the pain of now and the pain of then*, you will slowly come to understand how you thought you had to choose the current situation because deep inside you could not possibly admit "defeat." Once this happens, the insight you gain, the experience you feel exactly as I say here, will enable you to take the next step.

It goes without saying that many people are not even aware of any pain, past or present. They busily push it out of sight. Their problems do not appear as "pain." For them, the very first step is to become aware that this pain is present and that it hurts infinitely more as long as they have not become aware of it. Many people are afraid of this pain and like to believe that by ignoring it they can make it disappear. They chose such a means of relief only because their conflicts have become too great for them. How much more wonderful it is for a person to choose this path with the wisdom and conviction that a hidden conflict, in the long run, does as much damage as a manifest one. They will not fear to uncover the real emotion and will feel, even in the temporary experience of acute pain, that in that moment it turns into a healthy growing pain, free of bitterness, tension, anxiety, and frustration.

There are also those who tolerate the pain, but in a negative way, always expecting it to be remedied from the outside. Such people are in a way nearer to the solution because for them it will be quite easy to see how the childish process still operates. The outside is the offending parent, or both parents, projected onto other human beings. They have only to redirect the approach to their pains. They do not have to find it.

How to Stop Re-creating?

Only after experiencing all these emotions, and synchronizing the "now" and the "then," will you become aware of how you tried to correct the situation. You will further see the folly of the unconscious desire to re-create the childhood hurt, the frustrating uselessness of it. You will survey all your actions and reactions with this new understanding and insight, whereupon you will release your parents. You will leave your childhood truly behind and start a new inner behavior pattern that will be infinitely more constructive and rewarding for you and for others. You will no longer seek to master the situation you could not master as a child. You will go on from where you are, forgetting and forgiving truly inside of you, without even thinking that you have done so. You will no longer need to be loved as you needed to be loved when you were a child. First you become aware that this is what you still wish, and then you no longer seek this kind of love. Since you are no longer a child, you will seek love in a different way, by giving it instead of expecting it. It must always be emphasized, however, that many people are not aware that they do expect it. Since the childish, unconscious expectation was so often disappointed, they made themselves give up all expectations and all desire for love. Needless to say, this is neither genuine nor healthy, for it is a wrong extreme.

To work on this inner conflict is of great importance for all of you, so that you gain a new outlook and further clarification in your self-search. At first these words may give you perhaps only an occasional glimpse, a temporary flickering emotion in you, but they should be of help and open a door toward knowing yourself better, toward evaluating your life with a more realistic and more mature outlook.

Now, are there any questions in connection with this lecture?

QUESTION: It is very difficult for me to understand that one continually chooses a love object who has exactly the same negative trends that one or the other parent had. Is it reality that this particular person has these trends? Or is it projection and response?

ANSWER: It can be both and it can be either. In fact, most of the time it is a combination. Certain aspects are unconsciously looked for and found and they are actually similar. But the existing similarities are enhanced by the person who is doing the recreation. They are not only projected qualities which are not really there, but are latent in some degree without being manifested. These are encouraged and strongly brought to the fore by the attitude of the person with the unrecognized inner problem. He or she fosters something in the other person by provoking the reaction that is similar to the parent's. The provocation, which of course is entirely unconscious, is a very strong factor here.

The sum total of a human personality consists of many aspects. Out of these, let us say three or four may be actually similar to some traits in the recreator's parent. The most outstanding would be a similar kind of immaturity and incapacity to love. That alone is sufficient and potent enough in essence to reproduce the same situation.

The same person would not react to others as he or she reacts to you because it is you who constantly do the provoking, thereby reproducing conditions similar to your childhood for you to correct. Your fear, your self-punishment, your frustration, anger, hostility, your withdrawal from giving out love and affection, all these trends of the child in you constantly provoke the other person and enhance a response coming from that part which is weak and immature. However, a more mature person will affect others differently and will bring out that in them which is mature and whole, for there is no person who does not have some mature aspects.

QUESTION: How can I make the distinction as to whether the other person provoked me or I the other person?

ANSWER: It is not necessary to find who started it, for this is a chain reaction, a vicious circle. It is useful to start by finding your own provocation, perhaps in response to an open or hidden provocation of the other person. Thus you will realize that because you were provoked, you provoke the other person. And because you do so, the other again responds in kind. But as you examine and understand your real reason, not the superficial one, the reason why you were hurt in the first place and therefore provoked, you will no longer regard this hurt as disastrous. You will have a different reaction to the hurt, and, as a consequence, the hurt will diminish automatically. Therefore, you will no longer feel the need to provoke the other person. Also, as the need to reproduce the childhood situation decreases, you will become less withdrawn and you will hurt others less and less so that they will not have to provoke you. If they do, you will now also understand that they reacted out of the same childish blind needs as you did. Now you can see how you ascribe different motivations to the other person's provocation than to your own, even if and when you actually realize that you initiated the provocation. As you gain a different view on your own hurt, understanding its real origin, you will gain the same detachment from the reaction of the other person. You will find exactly the same reactions in yourself and in the other. As long as the child's conflict remains unresolved in you, the difference seems enormous, but when you perceive reality, you begin to break the repetitive vicious circle.

As you truly perceive such a mutual interplay, it will relieve the feeling of isolation and guilt you all are burdened with. You are constantly fluctuating between your guilt and your accusation of injustice you direct at those around you. The child in you feels itself entirely different from others, in a world of its own. It lives in such a damaging illusion. As you solve this conflict, your awareness of other people will increase. As yet, you are so unaware of the reality of other people. On the one hand you accuse them and are inordinately hurt by them because you do not understand yourself and therefore do not understand the other person. On the other hand, and at the same time, you refuse to become aware when you are hurt. This seems paradoxical, yet is not. As you experience for yourself the interactions set forth tonight, you will find this to be true. While sometimes you may exaggerate a hurt, at other times you do not allow yourself to know that it happened at all, because it may not fit the picture you have of the situation. It may spoil your self-constructed idea, or it may not correspond to your desire at the time. If the situation seems otherwise favorable and fits into your preconceived idea, you leave out all that jars you, allowing it to fester underneath and create unconscious hostility. This entire reaction inhibits your intuitive faculties, at least in this particular respect.

The constant provocation that goes on among human beings, while it is hidden from your awareness now, is a reality you will come to perceive very clearly. This will have a very liberating effect on you and your surroundings. Go your way, my dearest ones, and may the blessings we bring to all of you envelop and penetrate your body, soul, and spirit, so that you open up your soul and become your real self, your own real self. Be blessed, my friends, be in peace, be in God.

Attachment of the Life Force to Negative Situations

Greetings, my dearest friends. Blessings for every one of you. May the strength contained in these blessings aid you in assimilating this lecture, not only with your outer, but also with your inner understanding.

Why do destructiveness, illness, war and cruelty continue to exist? Let me explain what is missing from the answers that have been given to these questions.

I have often said that misconceptions—wrong, unconscious conclusions about life—create strife, and this is perfectly true. But there is an additional element without which no misconception could have power. It is this: Undiluted negativity, as in an overtly destructive attitude, has much less of an effect than destructiveness attached to and combined with the positive life principle. This is what makes manifestations on this earth plane particularly serious or severe. In other words, when a positive life force mingles with a negativity or a destructive attitude, *this combination creates evil*. Real destructiveness comes, therefore, not only from a distortion of truth, but from a distortion that is permeated with the universal life principle and its constructive power. If the positive life principle were not also involved, then evil, or destructiveness, would be of very short duration.

The dynamic life force is particularly available to human consciousness in the love relationship between the sexes. When your striving or longing for this experience is attached to a negative condition, difficulty and frustration must follow. Look at yourself from the following point of view: All of you have endured certain hurts and pains as a child. Some of you may have begun to grasp, if ever so slightly, that at the moment when you were hurt a specific process took place. *The erotic, or pleasure principle, was put in the service of your hurt, your suffering, your pain.* All the emotions arising from this original hurt, according to character and temperament, also combine with the pleasure principle. This attachment creates all the personal difficulties, all the unwelcome circumstances.

The Combination of Cruelty and Pleasure

The many souls inhabiting this earth, added together, create the general strife of humankind. When you realize, after having become aware of this process, how many people can experience pleasure combined with fantasies of cruelty, you will understand that here is the actual nucleus of war—of cruelty itself. This should not make you feel guilty. It should rather enlighten you and free you to allow your inner processes to transform, now that you know what has created this condition. Cruelty without the pleasure principle could never have real power. Lack of awareness of the combination of cruelty and pleasure by no means alleviates the effect it has on the overall climate of humanity's emanation.

If you have experienced cruelty, whether the act of cruelty was an actual fact or a creation of your imagination, your pleasure principle is attached to it and functions to some extent in connection with cruelty. Often the guilt and shame are so strong that the entire fantasy life is denied, but sometimes it is conscious. Awareness of this must be established and understood from an overall point of view, for if it is truly understood, both guilt and shame will be removed. As understanding grows, the pleasure principle will gradually respond to positive events.

The combination between the pleasure principle and cruelty can operate either actively or passively. Therefore, pleasure is experienced either in inflicting cruelty or in enduring it—or both. Attaching the pleasure principle to a condition where it functions most strongly in conjunction with cruelty creates a holding back from love, limits it, and makes the actual experience of love impossible. Love exists only as a vague yearning that cannot be maintained or followed through. Under these circumstances love is not the tempting, pleasurable experience it may be to another part of the personality. The yearning for the pleasure of love and the ignorance about the fact that one rejects its actual experience because one fears the attachment of the pleasure principle to negativity, often creates a deep hopelessness. The hopelessness can be understood and instantly relieved only when this particular fact is profoundly comprehended.

In less crass cases, when the child experiences not so much outright cruelty, but vague rejection or nonacceptance, the pleasure principle will attach itself to a similar situation, so that in spite of the conscious desire for acceptance, the pleasure current will only be activated in conjunction with rejection. There are many degrees and variations of this, for example, situations where a child experiences partial acceptance and partial rejection. Then the pleasure principle is attached to an exactly similar ambivalence. This, then, creates a conflict in actual relationships.

The first, crass instance of *attaching cruelty to the pleasure principle* or the life principle—they are both the same—*will make a relationship so hazardous that it is often avoided altogether.* Or the discovery of this combination is so puzzling and frightening that you are incapable of continuing the relationship. Or, you are inhibited because the shame of the desire for either inflicting or enduring cruelty may prohibit all spontaneity and make you withdraw from and numb all feelings.

My dearest friends, this is a tremendously important principle to understand. It applies to humanity as a whole as well as to the individual. Generally, it has not been sufficiently understood because psychology and spiritual science have not merged sufficiently. Vague attempts have been made by psychology to grasp this factor, and it has been understood in some measure, but the vast significance in terms of civilization and its fate, or its evolution, is not understood. The world is now ready to understand this fact of life.

Evolution Comes About by Inner Change

Evolution, my friends, means that each individual, through the process of personal self-confrontation and self-realization, gradually changes the inner orientation of the pleasure principle. In their spontaneous reactions, more and more individuals will respond to positive events, situations, conditions.

You all know that such inner change cannot be willed directly. The direct expression of your will must go in the direction of sustained work on a spiritual path such as this. Cultivate the will and the courage to look at the self to find and overcome resistance to self-understanding. As you use your will and your ego faculties in this constructive manner, the real change happens, almost as though it had nothing to do with your efforts, as if it were an unconnected unfoldment. This is the way progress and growth must happen.

Gradually, through the process of growth, one individual after another reorients the soul movements, the soul forces. The expression of the cosmic movement within the psyche will then attach itself to purely positive conditions. Positive or pleasurable feelings will no longer be derived from negative circumstances.

Now you still repress and suppress awareness of the combination of pleasurable feelings with something negative. Instead of repressing it, denying it, looking away from it, you must face it. Understand it without guilt or shame. In the course of growing you learn that all imperfection must be courageously accepted and understood before it can be changed.

The "Marriage" Between the Pleasure Current and a Negative Condition

My friends, try to find your specific inner "marriage" between the pleasure current and a negative condition. As you find this marriage within your own soul forces in specific terms, you will know and perfectly understand certain outer manifestations of your problems. This will be a relief. Through clearly seeing and formulating the marriage of positive and negative forces in your psyche, you will understand the exact image of your unfulfillment. To what extent does this manifest—perhaps only in your fantasies—and how does this hold you back from self-expression, from union, from experience, from a fearless state of self-realization with a kindred spirit? You will see why you keep yourself hidden from yourself and from life; why you withdraw from your own feelings; why you repress and why you stand guard over the most spontaneous and creative forces within yourself. You will see why you block out feelings, sometimes with a great amount of pain, then try to rationalize and explain them away.

Now, are there any questions in connection with this topic?

QUESTION: I would like to understand a little more concretely about the marriage between the forces of love and cruelty. For instance, in the case of a child who feels rejected by his mother, does this marriage mean that he cannot experience pleasure without also experiencing revenge—some kind of sadistic wish toward the mother? This happens perhaps only in fantasy, never in reality, and then the person is usually unaware that the partner represents the mother?

ANSWER: Yes, it might be exactly that. Or it might also be that pleasure can be experienced only in connection with being rejected again, or a little rejected, or being fearful that rejection may occur.

QUESTION: But he didn't experience pleasure when he was rejected.

ANSWER: Of course not. But the child uses the pleasure principle to make the negative event, the suffering, more bearable. This happens unconsciously, unintentionally, and almost automatically. Inadvertently, as it were, the pleasure principle combines with the negative condition. The automatic reflexes are then geared to a situation that combines the inherent pleasure current with the painful event. The only way this can be individually determined is by investigating one's fantasy life.

QUESTION: So the child wishes to reproduce the rejection?

ANSWER: Not consciously, of course. No one really wants to be rejected. The trouble is that people consciously wish to be accepted and loved, but unconsciously they cannot respond to a completely accepting and favorable situation. In such cases the pleasure principle has already been diverted into the negative channel and can be rechanneled only through awareness and understanding. It is the very nature of this conflict that the pleasure principle functions in exactly the opposite way people consciously would want it to. One cannot say that a person unconsciously desires rejection, but the reflex is already established from the time when this way of functioning made life more bearable for the child. Do you understand that?

QUESTION: I don't quite understand how pleasure can be experienced at all when someone is rejected, except in the form of revenge. That I can understand.

ANSWER: Perhaps you can imagine also—one sees this over and over again—that when people feel too secure in being accepted and loved, they lose the spark of interest. This, too, they rationalize by claiming that the spark inevitably gets lost through habit, or invent other such subterfuges. But it would not have to be that way if it were not for the factors discussed in this lecture. With the attachment of the life force to something negative, the spark, the interest, the dynamic flow exists only when there is an insecure or an unhappy situation. You see this frequently. Sometimes the negative condition manifests only in fantasy. These fantasies are, in one way or another, attached to suffering, humiliation, or hostility. This is then called masochism or sadism.

QUESTION: When will there be an end to this situation? It always repeats itself in each incarnation.

ANSWER: You can see that there are differences among human beings: Some function in a much healthier way, and their pleasure principle responds more strongly to a positive situation. There evolution is taking place. When a completely positive situation exists in the psyche, reincarnation is no longer necessary. Evolution then proceeds on other levels. To a certain degree, every human being has negativity, and this negativity is somehow activated, enforced, and nourished by the life force. But degrees exist, and they are a clear indication of the evolutionary process.

Fantasy and Reality Can Be Brought Together

You have human beings, at one extreme, who cannot even have any direct relationship with another person, who live merely in fantasies that are utterly attached to negative experiences. At the other extreme are those who, in the process of maturing, have brought together fantasy and reality in the most positive and favorable sense. This bringing together of fantasy and reality does not mean repression of fantasy life, but true overcoming of it, because reality is more desirable and more pleasurable, just as positive circumstances are. Between the two poles, many degrees exist. You can see the evolutionary process.

In this connection I would like to add one more point, not just for you, but generally. It is also useful, my friends, to distinguish between two prevalent reactions to this conflict. Both of them are mostly unconscious. The first is strict denial so that no awareness of any negativity exists even in fantasy. This comes from fear, guilt, and shame. The second applies to those who are perfectly aware of their fantasies but are unable to experience the pleasure principle in any other way, whether or not they actually have relationships with others. It occurs when sexuality and love are separated, or eros and love, or eros and sexuality. In these cases, a semi-conscious resistance to giving up the fantasy life exists out of fear that the pleasure will be lost altogether. The person cannot conceive that the pure, healthy pleasure principle manifests much more beautifully and satisfyingly when positive melds with positive. One imagines that this would be dull and boring, because with this conflict, the actual, real-life relationship is never as satisfying as the fantasy. Hence, one assumes that giving up the fantasy means giving up the pleasure, and, of course, one does not wish to part with one's pleasure.

Two Kinds of Guilt

Another point I should like to make tonight is about *guilt feelings*. As I said before, everybody has guilt. Every image is interwoven with guilt. It is important to understand that *there are two kinds of guilt*—unjustified guilt and justified guilt. Often you unconsciously use an absurd, unjustified guilt as a shield and hide the true guilt behind it. Why? Because deep down you know that the unjustified guilt is ridiculous. It is as though you wanted to say, "You see, I declare myself guilty, but I have no real reason to do so." You cannot get rid of the gnawing voice of that which should really be acknowledged, faced, and changed. Yet you do not want to face it, hence you look unconsciously for something you cannot be blamed for. Thus you argue with your inner voice of absurd guilt, trying to convince it that it has no reason to bother you. Of course, all this happens unconsciously. Ironically, the true guilt may be infinitely smaller than the absurd guilt you use as a wall to hide behind.

What are absurd guilts? They are most of all the guilts you feel because you are not perfect. It is commendable to want to become perfect. It cannot be recommended enough that you try to replace hatred, resentment, aggression with love and unselfishness. But before you can do that, you must first acknowledge and accept your present state of development— your inability to feel differently than you do—instead of wanting to immediately become more than you are now. If you feel guilty because you are still what you are, you obstruct the very goal you want to attain. I know, my friends, that I repeat many things many times, but I must do so. I want to stress that it is an unjustified guilt feeling when you blame yourself for not being perfect now. Such unjustified guilt extends into all areas of the human personality. Examine your guilt feelings from this viewpoint, and you will recognize this type of guilt in you.

Is Guilt About the Sexual Drive Justified?

Another unjustified guilt—fueled by a mass-image—is your reaction to your sexual drive. Each one of you feels guilty about it, if not on the surface, where you have been affected by intellectual influences, then certainly way down deep in your emotions. *Guilt about the sexual drive is unjustified, absurd guilt.* It may be true that your sexual energy does not flow in the right channel because it does not merge with love. That it does not is precisely because you have felt guilty about it and suppressed awareness of it as much as you could. Hence your sexual drive could not mature with the rest of your personality and integrate with warm, loving, giving, unselfish feelings. Instead, it has remained childish in its self-directedness and egotism.

Your unconscious sexual fault lies in the *misdirection and separateness of your sexual drive* rather than in its existence as such. Its existence is no reason for feeling guilty. You act on a misunderstanding when you attempt to eliminate that which seems sinful to you, and then feel guilty because you cannot do so. The remedy is not to eliminate the sexual drive but to cease to be afraid of love—to relinquish a fear that is selfish in nature. If you allow yourself to love, your sexual drive will merge with your love, and there will no longer be any reason to feel guilty about your sexuality. Try to understand that, my dear friends. Try to understand how confused your unconscious thinking is. *You feel guilty about a God-given force instead of feeling guilty about your fear of loving, which is born of selfishness and separateness. Combine your sexual drive with the one and only reality and remedy in the universe—love.* You can combine love and sexual energy only by developing your soul, as on the very path you are taking.

What Kind of Guilt is Justified?

What, on the other hand, is justified guilt? When you hurt other people in your ignorant belief that selfishness is your protection—whether you hurt them actively or passively, by commission or omission—*then your guilt is justified.* Differentiate clearly, my dear friends, between the guilt of present imperfection and the guilt of hurtful selfwill. Being imperfect should not in itself make you feel guilty. But the guilt for hurts you inflict on others, no matter how unintentionally—out of your imperfection, blindness, and ignorance—is justified guilt that you should meet squarely and courageously. There is a world of difference, although fine and subtle, between the two types of guilt I have described. Please think about this. It is so important.

What should your attitude be toward justified guilt? What would be healthy and constructive? It would be to say to yourself, "I could not help it in the past. I was ignorant and blind and selfish. I was too much of a coward to dare to love and forget my own little ego. I admit that I have hurt other people by this attitude and I am now willing to learn exactly how I hurt them. It makes no difference whether I inflicted the hurt by deed, word, thought, or emotional reaction, by what I have done or left undone. I truly want to change. With the help of God I will succeed. To do so, I must clearly see the direct or indirect hurts my attitude has inflicted upon others." Then think about the hurts you inflicted. Pray for the insight to understand. Have the courage to shoulder your responsibility without the pride of destructive wrong guilt feelings that make you exaggerate your own "badness" and lead you to feel hopeless about yourself.

The three possible wrong reactions as you recognize the hurts you have inflicted on others are: *hopelessness* about yourself—the negative, destructive guilt feelings that make you despair of yourself; *self-justification*—the blaming of others for real or imagined wrongs that "forced" you to react that way; and *denial*—the fearful refusal to look at imperfection which may not fit into the picture you have of yourself. At different times you may experience any one of these reactions. Beware of each! Find the right way: feel with the person you have hurt, take the justified guilt upon yourself, wish to become different, desire to give up your fear of loving. Such attitude is healthy and constructive. The hurt you feel when you realize the hurt you have unwittingly inflicted—unintentional hurt because it was committed out of your wrong image conclusions—is healthy: it will give you the incentive to lose your fear and your selfishness. It will foster a healthy and constructive inner movement. It will set the life force in motion in your soul. For, among many other things, life force is truth and courage.

There is no doubt, my dearest ones, that everyone of you who truly wishes will find more and more the beauty, the peace, the dynamic life and inner security that exist in the self-realization you have begun to cultivate. You will experience moments of living in the eternal now of yourself, instead of striving away from it. Each *now* must bring you answers. If you recall this simple fact in your meditations, in your approach to yourself, your meditations will become more fruitful as you go on. What you have to look forward to in the time to come will be even more liberating than what you have already begun to experience.

Be blessed, be in peace, be in God.

Life,
Love and Death

Greetings, my dearest friends. Blessings for each one of you. Blessed be your every effort in the direction of self-development, liberation, and self-realization.

One of the fundamental human predicaments is the struggle to overcome the duality between life and death. From this basic predicament derive all other problems, difficulties, fears, and tensions you have to contend with. Whether this manifests directly as fear of death, of aging, or of the unknown, it is always *fear of the passing of time.*

To assuage these fears, humanity has created philosophical, spiritual, religious concepts. But concepts, even if they originate from someone's true experience, will not relieve the tension. The only way to overcome fear and reconcile the great duality is to delve into the first unknown you fear so much: your own psyche.

The Great Unknown

To the degree you are unaware of what goes on within you, you will fear the "great unknown." When one is young, these fears may be assuaged. But sooner or later every human being will be confronted more directly with the fear of death. I want to emphasize again: to the degree that you know yourself, you fulfill yourself, your life, your dormant potential. And to that degree death will not be feared but experienced as an organic development. The unknown will no longer pose a threat.

One of the main obstacles to overcoming the fear of death is *the fear of letting go of the barriers which separate you from the opposite sex.* There is a very direct connection between these three: fear of one's own unconscious, fear of love with the opposite sex, and fear of death. Once you experience these connections yourself, in the effort of self-understanding, you will know the truth of these words.

Self-fulfillment depends on fulfilling yourself as a man or as a woman, respectively. Ultimately, you cannot fulfill yourself without overcoming the barrier between you and the opposite sex, thus truly becoming a man or a woman. Of course, there are also other aspects of self-fulfillment. You may be unaware of certain potentials you possess: your talents, your strengths, your inherent good qualities, such as your courage and resourcefulness, your broadmindedness, your creativity. However, none of these can truly unfold in their inherent splendor unless a man truly becomes a man, and a woman truly becomes a woman. The self-realization that takes place while the barrier to union with a mate still remains can be only partial and conditional. For this barrier indicates a resistance to fully grown selfhood and an insistence on artificial infancy.

When all resistance to unknown areas in oneself has vanished so that one no longer fears oneself, one cannot possibly fear other human beings, including the opposite sex. A great inner freedom and trust, born out of an objective, realistic attitude releases the tight grip of control that stands in the way of *letting oneself go into the state of being.* When you fulfill yourself, there is no longer a barrier, no more holding on in fear of the unknown, in distrust of the self or the other. The same holding on prevents you from entering into the cosmic stream of timelessness that you experience in the highest bliss of union with a mate, and that you experience in the highest bliss in what you call death.

Death has many faces. Those who are afraid, tightly holding onto the little self, may experience death as fearful seclusion and separateness, but for those who are not afraid of living fully, of reaching out and no longer preserving the little self, death is the glory that union on this earth can be and more! *Therefore, the struggle of self-realization, in the last analysis, must lead to: first, removal of the barriers between your consciousness and the hidden areas of your psyche.* These hidden areas are not always covered up and unconscious—they are often right in front of your eyes if you but choose to look at them. *Second, removal of the barriers between you and your counterpart,* whoever he or she may be at a given phase. And the *third barrier is between you and the cosmic stream.* Whenever this stream carries you, you will experience its rightness. It is functional, it is organic. But those who fear themselves, the other, and therefore the stream of being, do not trust the passing of time. They hold on tightly to the little self, creating a wall of clouds between their momentary awareness and their higher consciousness.

Three Basic Hindrances to Self-Expression

The three basic hindrances are *pride, selfwill, and fear. All conflicts derive from these three basic human faults. The same triad barricades access to the three avenues of self-expansion.* Let us consider this more closely.

Take first the barrier between consciousness and the unconscious.

Pride bars the way because you fear that you may not like what you will find if you venture into the unknown within yourself. It may not be flattering or compatible with your idealized self-image. This creates a block of pride that hinders insight.

Selfwill separates the conscious from the unconscious in you because you are apprehensive that what you find may force you to do something that your little ego is not inclined to do, or to give up something which it is unwilling to surrender. Selfwill wants the little ego to be in control, so you can cling to the known.

Fear bars the way when both pride and selfwill indicate a lack of trust; then fear makes you believe that the final reality is not to be trusted. Cosmic reality is embedded in your deep unconscious as the stream of cosmic events. If you enter into this stream, it cannot help but be benign, bringing happiness, fulfillment, and meaning to your life. Distrusting this stream and therefore holding on to what you know, in the belief that you might fare better than by taking the chance of entering the unknown, creates walls of fear. It is this fear that blocks full self-recognition.

The triad of pride, selfwill, and fear also applies to the barrier between the self and a mate.

Pride enters because, whether you are man or woman, you fear the apparent helplessness—and therefore shame—of giving over to a force greater than your little ego. Love between the sexes is a humbling experience and therefore the enemy of pride. Your pride wants to direct and control; it does not want to give over to any force, even if this force is most desirable. Even though you and everyone else go through life desiring to love, you still block it and find ways to strike a compromise with those contradictory currents in your soul which continue to resist it. The force driving you into love is great indeed, for it derives from your innermost nature. Yet, the drive of pride, selfwill, and fear pushes you away from love.

Selfwill is opposed to love because it wants to control everything; it cannot give itself up. It seems to you—erroneously, of course—that only when you obey and are governed by the little self are you safe. You are under the misapprehension that giving yourself over to the love force is the same as heedless and headless lack of realism. This is not so. Realism, objectivity, the ability to relinquish, and fearless willingness to enter love are not only compatible but interdependent. You block out the love experience for fear of losing your dignity—meaning pride—and your selfhood— meaning selfwill—when, in reality, true dignity and selfhood can be gained only by giving up pride and selfwill.

The *fear* of losing one's very life is not so different from the fear that blocks the blissful experience of self-forgetfulness in union with a mate. Some of you may sense the similarity, at least occasionally.

The triad of pride, selfwill, and fear also influence one's attitude to death. Dying ultimately means giving up self-direction—and this surrender, strange as this may seem, appears humiliating. In order to avoid the humbling truth that the little self is not all-powerful, you hold onto it in pride and selfwill, thereby creating ever stronger waves of fear.

In order to resolve the conflict between giving up the self and full possession of the self, I would like to pose a question that may indeed sound like a paradox: are you finding yourself on such a laborious path of self-realization only to become capable of giving yourself up to union with the other sex and to death? The truth is that you cannot give up successfully what you have not found, for you cannot freely let go of something you have never really possessed. Only when you can freely give up your selfhood will you gain more selfhood.

Now, if death, or dying, can be such a blissful experience, why then is it perceived so darkly? Why doesn't a death instinct, a yearning for death exist, as, for example, the strong instinct to lose oneself in love? Why must death be encountered without the help of instinctual drives, and why must human beings work so hard to overcome the barrier of fear? You may ask, why is it that we, on this earth, have to battle against this great unknown?

Why is There No Death-Instinct?

At first glance, such questions seem justified and logical, but when you take a closer look, you will understand that things must be as they are. You see, my friends, it would be so easy to wish for death because you cannot cope with life when life is painful and unfulfilling. In this unfinished, ignorant, and blind state of terror, you would all too easily escape into death—even though, in this case, death would not prove any different than life, for both are intrinsically the same. In order to avoid such a destructive escape, the life instinct must be very strong, and it can operate only as long as death remains an unknown. Words cannot remove your fear of the unknown, but your life instinct can prevent you from choosing death out of negative, destructive motivations. This strengthens the stamina to try and try again, until life is finally mastered through understanding the self, and hence the universe. Then the inner understanding will finally dawn that death is not to be feared—or, that it is feared only in exact proportion to the still existing fear of living and loving. Hence the sharp cleavage between life and death, their illusory opposition, begins to dwindle. You will not need to rush ahead, nor will you need to hold back.

If you look at your conscious and unconscious attitudes toward the passage of time, toward life and death, you will find that they are identical with one another and with your innermost, hidden attitudes toward love, regardless of your conscious, healthy desires. You will find that the fear of the unknown plays a role in all these attitudes. You will find that you constantly fluctuate between trying to hold back time in a fear-cramped motion and rushing ahead because you cannot stand the moment. Very rarely indeed are you in harmony with the cosmic stream of your life, your individuality. This is what being in peace with oneself, being in harmony with God, really means: not holding back, not pushing toward, but dissolving in the life stream, in full possession of yourself, yet without fear of giving up self-possession. This is the great experience that you are blessed and privileged to have when you find your mate. And this will ultimately be the experience of going into a new form of consciousness.

The Key Lies in Self-Discovery

When you avoid looking at some parts of yourself, you cannot help but *project outwardly* onto others and into the outside life what is in you. Projection cannot yield peace and liberation, regardless of how much precarious temporary satisfaction it appears to give. Often it is not easy to recognize in what respect fear of self and of life exists in you. It may manifest only through symptoms. Look for the symptoms and investigate them for their significance. Take for example your attitude to your work on your path, professed and actual; your attitude to the opposite sex—again professed and actual; your reactions to current life circumstances. All this has to be looked at with a penetrating spirit of truthfulness. When you can determine a fear of, or to use a more psychological term, resistance to, your innermost self, you can be sure that fear of death must exist in equal measure. And so does the fear of loving, of letting go of yourself in this great experience. Find it, see it in yourself, and you will have conquered a great deal.

Each little step in the right direction will eventually dissolve the clouds, the barriers, between you and the timeless stream of higher consciousness. This consciousness furnishes you with all the wisdom, truth, and rightness you need for your everyday life. Some of you have occasionally tapped this source and experienced it, only to lose it again. When you contact the inner source of peace, truth, and highest bliss, you will deeply comprehend the significance of Creation.

Truth is like the sun, around which all other planets revolve, while it remains constant and bright, even though it is often covered by clouds. The clouds are your pride, your selfwill, and your fear, your ignorance and your stemming against, or hurrying ahead of, time. But in the moments you perceive your truth—be it ever so banal or apparently insignificant in terms of cosmic development—the clouds disperse and the warm sun of your higher consciousness regenerates you with strength and well-being, with joyfulness and peace. This sun within yourself is constantly ready to warm and enliven you, but you, my dearest ones, must overcome much more. Then all fears, all pride, and all selfwill will fall away. If they already had, many of your reactions, feelings, and expressions, as well as the effect you have on others and they on you, would be drastically different.

The Eternal Now

This is not an easy topic. It needs more than a search for understanding with your mind, which, in itself, will accomplish little. It needs the keener understanding of your being, which can come only when you look at the feelings that keep you from happiness at this moment. If you look at your desires, fears, and needs, your apprehensions and reactions—right or wrong—at this and every moment, you will find the eternal now. In it you can live fearlessly with rightful confidence in the unknown. You do not have to become perfect; you are perfect, in a sense, when you can calmly face, acknowledge, and come to terms with your present imperfection.

When you no longer struggle against the self, shedding your pride and pretense, and become willing to change, you also shed your selfwill, together with all fears of self, of others, of life, of love and of dying—all these evaporate like ice in the sun.

Blessings for each one of you. Do not despair, my friends, when you sense the barriers I discussed tonight. They are removed more effectively through awareness of their existence than through ignorance. Please realize and understand this important truth. Make it your own by testing it, and you will rejoice. Be blessed in this new awareness, each one of you. Be in peace, be in yourself, and therefore in God!

From Unconscious Negative Interaction to Conscious Choice of Love

Greetings and blessings for every one of my beloved friends. The power of love and the strength of truth will unfold in you forever more as you grow on your path.

In this lecture I will show you what the *unconscious* psychic interaction between you and others means in terms of the *loss of love.*

When you are only vaguely aware of your negativity, dimly sensing the hurt that it inflicts on others, you are caught in a battle between blame and self-justification. You cannot help but hook others—with their own unconscious conflicts—into your negativity. By denying your negativity you incur a double guilt. First, there is the guilt for the negative attitude itself. This we may call the *primary guilt.* When you deny the negativity, you get involved in what we may call the *secondary guilt.* If the primary guilt were admitted and the consequences of what caused it truly accepted, it would cease to be a guilt. But the secondary guilt must weigh heavily on everyone's soul. It is a burden that consumes much vital life energy. Your denial always implies inner or outer harmful acts toward others; you punish others for your own failings, negative intentions, lovelessness, untruthfulness, spite, and unfair demands.

If you are aware, for instance, that you do not wish to love and you do not pretend otherwise, this is your responsibility. If you realize that you pay a heavy price for a loveless existence, but you let it go at that, at least you do not hook others into your guilt for not loving. You will be alone, of course, but you have made a choice; you know it and you pay the price for it. You withhold from the world your wonderful love capacity, that is true, and in that sense you fail.

Blaming Others

But when you blame others for your lack of love, even if you use their real shortcomings as your excuse, when you punish them for the result of your own unloving attitude and build cases in order to justify your own holding back, then you truly do harm, my friends.

This process is most widespread, most common, and yet so subtle that only people who possess a considerable amount of self-awareness can begin to recognize it in themselves, and therefore also in others. It is a basic attitude. It exists in many variations and with different degrees of intensity. The refusal to love, when not admitted, often manifests in the following attitude: "I do not want to give you anything—whoever "you" may be—but I demand that you give me everything. If you do not, I will punish you." This attitude is very typical. The more concealed and the less consciously expressed it is, the more insidious its effect will be on the self and others. It is always relatively easy to deny, rationalize, distort, conceal, or use half-truths to justify this attitude.

When you have become aware of this attitude in yourself and can admit it also to your friends, the influx of health, of the clean fresh air of psychic truth, is instantaneous: you have freed yourself from the secondary guilt. The more you expose every detail of the disparity between your demands, your own ungiving intentions and the punishment you mete out when your demands are not met, the more you clear yourself of guilt. The clearer you can see the unfairness of what you demand compared to what you give, how differently you insist on being treated from how you treat others, and exactly how you choose to punish—always so that you cannot be caught, so you cannot be made accountable—the quicker you will free yourself of a burden that causes depression, anxiety, worry, hopelessness, and often physical illness and material frustration as well.

One of the most popular ways of punishing others for not responding with love to your ungivingness is to render them guilty—to build your case in such a way that they seem to be the cause of your misery. You can convince yourself quite successfully of this when you choose to see only the result of your spiteful withholding. You deliberately ignore the fact that you cannot get the response that you would like from others when your own psyche is still steeped in a negative, non-giving attitude toward life.

Your negativity says, "I will deny the truth and will blame the other for not giving me all and for not letting me get away with my one-sided demands. And if he dare to react to this I will punish him by hating him and by blaming him even more." Those who are at the beginning of their path or who have a very strong investment in their idealized self-image, which makes no room for this truth, will first think it impossible that they, too, could harbor such an attitude. The best gauge to determine whether or not it exists in you is the state of your own mind and emotions. If you feel no anxiety and are comfortable with others, if your life is expanding in a joyous way, and if you regard occasional difficulties as meaningful stepping stones, then you have already vastly overcome this poisonous attitude. But you, too, must have had it at one time and dealt with it by working your way through your pride, your investment in your pretense, your cowardice.

When you admit your ill will, my friends, you perform the most fundamental act of love, whether you know it or not. If you do not admit your negative intent, you may give a lot, but never the real thing that counts most. You may give things, money, good deeds, even tenderness and concern, but they are hollow gifts without setting the other free by the honest admission of your negativity.

The guilt caused by your unfair demands, your spite, the withholding of your love, and the compounded guilt caused by punishing others for your misery, must erode your strength and your self-expression. It makes you truly weak. How can you, as long as you continue in this attitude, ever have faith in yourself, ever believe in your dignity as a free human being? You may try all sorts of artificial ways to instill self-confidence in yourself, but it will never work unless you face the secondary guilt and give it up by admitting it. Then you may even stay, if you so choose, with the primary guilt—the guilt of not wanting to love—but at least you have assumed the responsibility.

You see, my friends, yours is a world of duality. So much confusion exists because of the either/or alternative. Humanity is stymied by the dualistic concept that either one should be blamed—for whatever it may be—or the other person should. Either you are bad and wrong or the other person is. This creates a serious predicament, making it impossible to be in truth. If you are wrong and the other person blameless, you feel that there is something not quite right about the situation. You feel also that an undue responsibility is placed on you. If you are the one to assume the sole burden of the blame, you surely expect to be ostracized. This assumption is an unbearable load; it is untrue and does not permit clarity. It makes you feel even more inferior and unlovable. Your misery seems a just punishment rather than a choice you are free to alter whenever you so decide. By assuming the sole blame, you give permission, as it were, to others to secretly act out their own negative intentions.

Or, conversely, if you have to be completely justified in explaining your behavior, then you also put yourself in a terrible predicament: you again feel there is something wrong; you know that making the other all bad does not fit the truth either. If you have to protect this pretense, which may seem desirable in order to whitewash yourself of guilt, you will become anxious, afraid, threatened with having your defenses penetrated—so you cannot afford to be relaxed, natural, and close to others. Your stake in your "innocence" prevents intimacy. Again, you cannot feel right.

Unconscious Interaction

Most human beings are still incapable of experiencing how their distortion and negativity directly affects, reinforces, and hooks into the distortions and negativities of others. In the interaction between two psyches, the following takes place. Suppose your unspoken message to whoever you are hooked up with in a negative interaction is, "I will punish you for not fulfilling my insatiable demands. I will not love you or give you anything. I will punish you by making you guilty, and if you want something from me, I will not give it to you. I punish you most effectively by making myself the victim, so you cannot blame or catch me." Suppose the other person is inwardly struggling with giving up a similar stance. That person's resistance says, in turn, "I must not give up my defensive attitude. Others are out to hurt, to victimize, to exploit me. If I open my heart to love, I will get nothing but rejection, unfairness and hate in return. It does not pay. I had better remain closed up." Just imagine how your self-victimizing attitude will reinforce the irrational resistance of the other person to being open, vulnerable, and loving. The frightened part of the soul, which "protects" itself by negativity and withholding, will be reinforced considerably in this struggle whenever it encounters someone else's negative intentionality. The punishment often takes the form of severe accusations that malign the other's character. Or you may even use others' real failings as excuses to punish them for not living up to your demands and for not accepting a deal from you in which they give everything and you little or nothing.

The unconscious interaction in this area thus fortifies and justifies the conviction that negativity is a necessary defense. Viewed from this narrow vantage point, the position seems right. Thus when your intentions are negative, you are also responsible for the other. One of the apparently paradoxical truths of spiritual reality is that though you are primarily responsible for yourself, you are also responsible for the other, in a different way. By the same token, others' negative intentionality hurts you, and they are responsible for it to you.

Yet they could not succeed if you would not tenaciously hold on to your own. In that sense, the responsibility is yours. *Everyone has the choice of either using the other's bad intentions as an excuse for not loving, or looking for a new way of responding to life.* It is therefore equally correct to say that you are exclusively responsible for yourself and others are exclusively responsible for themselves, and that, ultimately, everyone is also responsible for the other person.

No Division in Ultimate Reality

Ultimately there is no division between the self and the other. You are the other and the other is you. The separation is an illusion. Therefore, when you end the old pattern of blaming others in order to justify your unfairness and your unloving demands, you not only unhook yourself from this double-bind, you also help unhook the other person. Of course others should not depend on you to do this; they must fend for themselves and find their own salvation. "Others should not depend on my overcoming my negativities and problems so that they can overcome theirs," you may say. And you are both right and wrong. You are right in that others can indeed do whatever they want, no matter what you do. Their efforts, investment and commitment to that will determine the outcome, regardless of what others, including you, do. But you are also wrong in not seeing that by your act of truth, which is an act of love, you help set the other free of his or her struggle. When you acknowledge your part, you remove a great deal of confusion, so that the true picture of how each party contributes to a negative psychic interaction can emerge. This has a tremendously liberating effect.

Just imagine how you would feel if someone close to you, who has given you pain by pointing out your real and your false guilts, but who has also confused you by the denial of his or her guilt, suddenly said to you: "I realize that I do not want to give you love. I want to demand from you and then blame you, accuse you, and punish you when you do not comply with my demands. But I do not allow you to feel hurt, because although

I want to hurt you, I do not want to be made to feel guilty by your hurt." Can you feel how this would set you free? It is unlikely that you would respond to such an act of love by being self-righteous, declaring that you have always known this, and establishing yourself as the innocent victim.

If you admit your similar unfair demands, your fear to expose your feelings, and your negative intentionality, it may hurt your pride, but can truly not hurt you in any other way! The other who hears it has, in that moment, received a gift of love from you, even though you may still not want to love with your heart, with your feelings, with your inner being. But you have begun to love by being truthful.

By setting others free from the false guilt you have placed on them in order to conceal your own, you allow them to look at their own real guilt without self-devastation and without the painful inner struggle in which the mutual guilts and accusations are all confused. Release and clarification often lead to the solution of the deepest problems. It is as though the personality needed this "outer" grace, this helping hand. For the dishonest placing of guilt on others makes their true self-revelation almost impossible; it implies that if they admit guilt you are right in accusing them of being bad and being the cause of your misery. This is how people are hooked together in denial, guilt-projection, either/or struggle, confusion, and negative interactions. Someone must begin to separate the interlocking hooks and disentangle the knots.

Negative intentionality is a defense. It stems from the innate belief that the world cannot be trusted and the only way the self can protect itself is by being as mean as the world is supposed to be—or meaner. When you admit your ill will, you help others to begin to trust in the decency of the world of people. They can then begin to ponder, "Maybe life is not so dangerous, after all. Maybe I am not all alone in my hidden shame and guilt. Maybe I can let go. Maybe I, too, can admit these feelings without being held solely responsible." What a difference this would be in everybody's attitude toward life! How it would affect your spiritual position as a human entity!

The Positive Effects of Honesty

When you all work together in this honest way, your energy system must begin to change. Love is not a command issued by the will and the mind; it is not an abstraction; it is not emoting, a sentimental gesture. It is vigorous, assertive, and free. *Honesty is the most needed and most rare form of love among human beings.* Without honesty, the illusion will always remain that you are separate from others; that your interests are contradictory; that in order to protect your interests, you must defeat others, and vice versa.

Only when you know your own negativity, my friends, truly own up to it, assume responsibility for it and no longer project it onto others while distorting reality to be able to do so, will you suddenly gain new insight into other people, so that even when they do not admit it, you will know what is happening. And that, too, sets you free. This is why everyone who admits the worst in themselves inevitably feels elation, liberation, energy, hope, and light as the immediate result.

Spiritual growth brings you the gift of knowing the inside of other people: their thoughts, intentions, and feelings. This is not magic; it occurs naturally because in reality you and others are one. As you read your own mind accurately, you cannot help reading those of others—since in reality it is all one mind. Other people are a closed book only as long as you hide from your own mind. To be able to read others' minds would amount to dangerous magic if it came from an individual's psychic power. Such power could be abused. But whenever this ability grows organically as a byproduct of knowing your own inner makeup, it is natural and cannot be abused in the service of power drives and negativity.

Expansion into Higher Awareness

Whenever human beings unfold into a more expanded state they need different tools. Let us take the simple analogy of someone who runs a business. When the business is very small, the organization is appropriate to the size and purpose of the firm and is therefore harmonious. But when the business expands, the organization created for a small establishment no longer fits. If the owners were too rigid to make changes and persisted in holding on to the old, established way, they would either fail in the expanded enterprise, or would at least find it very difficult to operate.

The same law, my friends, applies to your inner expansion. As you grow and learn about yourself, and therefore about others and the world, you experience life in deeper and more varied ways—which is, after all, your reason for being incarnated. You learn to experience feelings which you have previously avoided, you are setting the stage, as it were, for an "expanded operation." In practical terms this means that attitudes which were once useful now become destructive and limiting.

On the path of evolution, entities grow in various ways and prepare the ground for necessary new attitudes toward life. Yet they can impede their expansion by refusing to give up certain obsolete attitudes. So now you must adapt yourselves to new ways of responding to the world, my friends, responding differently to other people's reactions toward you, and also to what happens within you. This will come about, first, by knowing that your old response is a conditioned reflex created to fit a smaller way of functioning in life. And, second, by questioning that reflex and the beliefs behind it. Last but not least—and this is the basic theme of tonight's lecture—by *choosing love, rather than separateness, as your way of being in the world.*

Again, this must not be a mere word that covers up many things you do not wish to admit. The choice for love must be put into action according to where you are inwardly. Admitting your negativity is always an act of love, whether it is done directly to the person with whom you have a conflict if this is possible, or to a helper who is not personally involved with your negativity. It is still an act of love toward the universe. Even while you still choose to stay with your negativity, my friends, contemplate that one day you will want to give it up in love for the universe, in love for yourself.

Love is the Key

If you do not open your heart, you must wither away. No matter how true some diagnosis may be, how many insights you have into the background, history and dynamics of a condition that gives trouble, unless you commit yourself to opening your heart, no real change can ever occur. You cannot be fulfilled, my friends, unless you let yourself feel from the heart. And it is no use pretending that you want to love, that you even do love, as long as you are frightened of feeling your feelings. To the degree that it is so, you hold back from loving.

You cannot be strong and courageous, you cannot love yourself, unless you love. It is equally true that only as you love others can you love yourself. The first step must be to be willing to love. You do not start loving simply because you so choose. *You have to call on the divine nature of your innermost core to give you the grace of loving.* The grace of God may manifest through you in making you open your heart and lose your fear of feelings, of being vulnerable. That is all you need. If you do not love, you have nothing. If you love, you have everything.

But if you love falsely, as a pretense, it is much, much less loving and much more deceptive and harmful than when you admit your hate. Admitting your hate is more loving than an apparently loving act that denies the hate. Think of this, my friends.

Healthy Anger Can Be an Expression of Love

QUESTION: What about anger? Do I understand correctly that it is sometimes a good thing to express it?

ANSWER: Yes. Healthy anger must occasionally be expressed in a well-integrated life. Healthy anger does not create inner disharmony. It is a great misunderstanding to ignore or deny this fact. The denial comes from the artificial holding together of one's inner forces and from superimposing forced, false goodness. It is a false belief born of fear and obedience that occasional anger never exists in a truly spiritually evolved person.

In the human realm, healthy anger is a necessity. Without anger, there would be no justice and no progress. The destructive forces would take over. Allowing this takeover to happen is weakness, not love; fear, not goodness; appeasing and encouraging abuse, not constructive living. It destroys harmony rather than furthering it. It destroys healthy growth.

Anger can be as healthy and necessary an occasional reaction as love is. It forms part of love. It, too, comes spontaneously. It, too, cannot be forced. Trying to force or deny any emotion leads to self-deception which then may take the form of pretending that unhealthy anger is the healthy version.

The cause cannot determine whether the emotion elicited is healthy or unhealthy anger. The cause may entirely justify real, genuine, healthy anger which is, needless to say, constructive in this case. Yet, the anger experienced may be the unhealthy kind because of the personality's unresolved problems, insecurity, guilts and doubts, uncertainties and contradictions. The issue itself may warrant justified anger, but an individual may not be able to express that kind.

To the extent that an individual is capable of experiencing and expressing real love, to exactly that degree he or she is capable of manifesting constructive, healthy anger. Both real love and real anger come from the inner self. Absolutely any real feeling is healthy and constructive and furthers growth in the self and in others. Real feelings cannot be forced, commanded, or superimposed. They are a spontaneous expression, happening as an organic, natural result of self-confrontation.

QUESTION: In that case, would you permit physical violence?

ANSWER: No. Healthy anger does not necessarily manifest in physical violence. Expression of negative emotions, even when they are not healthy, need not in the least lead to destructive acts, either physically or otherwise.

This is one of the most frequent and hindering misconceptions. The inner psyche fears that acknowledgment of negative emotions must lead to acting them out. This is not so. On the contrary, you are free to choose whether or not to act, how and when, or to express any emotion only when you are fully aware. When you are not aware of what you really feel and why, you are constantly driven, and suffer from all sorts of compulsions you cannot understand. A compulsion is the direct result of unacknowledged, unconscious feelings and conditions. The more you know yourself, the more you are in control of your self. It is not, as you fear, "I cannot look at myself in candor because then I may have to let out undesirable impulses and do harm to others and therefore ultimately to myself." This apprehension also has to be brought to the surface to be dispelled.

Please repeat this in your daily meditation: "Awareness of what I feel, no matter how undesirable it may be, will make me free. I have choice of action only to the degree of my awareness. I can choose to verbally express my feelings when there is a good purpose, such as in a session with my helper. If I feel that such expression may impair a relationship, I will not do so, but will withhold it knowingly and without self-deception." Such meditation will strengthen you as it penetrates the hidden layers of your psyche. Healthy anger, since it comes from the real self, knows just what to do and how to meet the requirement of the moment.

Where there is fear of expressing a justified anger, there must also be fear of loving, which obstructs the manifestations of the real self, the outflow of genuine love as opposed to superimposed love, and of the capacity to express healthy anger as opposed to twisted, tortured anger. Healthy anger makes you stronger, twisted anger, weaker. Healthy love is all-embracing and enriches you the more you give out of yourself. Sickly, distorted, false love impoverishes and breeds conflict between self-interest and the interests of others. It comes from and increases duality; it always opposes the good to the bad. Ungenuine love is always connected with self-pity, resentment, hostility, and conflict. There is in it always the feeling of, "I ought to love, therefore I think I love, yet I do not want to love because then I will be taken advantage of. Since I ought to love and do not want to, I feel guilty and am bad." When you feel this way you cannot express healthy anger. It is dissipated at the source, for you doubt your right to feel anger, since you do not dare to love.

If you continue to struggle and to find the right expression of your feelings in the now, you must experience the beauty of the universe, the truth of being which knows no conflict. That truth combines loving with receiving one's full share of happiness. If you use goodwill to recognize that behind your trying to love lies a non-love born of fear, hurt, and illusion, then in the way of finding out what these illusions are, you must finally come to real love, your real self, the genuine expression of all you feel and are—which will be good and right.

Take the time to assimilate the material I have given to establish the most real and vital of all direct communications: that with your spiritual self. To do this, you must eliminate your self-deceptions and pretenses. They always block the way to God in you.

Those of you who have not yet found where and how they are unloving should set out to do so. Do not let yourself be deceived by the fact that in some part of yourself you are already loving. Ask yourself how fulfilled you feel in this love, how warm and unthreatened, how comfortable you feel in life. That will be your answer to how loving and how truthful you are. To the degree you admit your hate, punitiveness, or spitefulness, you start loving.

Understanding this, my friends, requires a lot of meditation and genuine goodwill. But then, what a key this is to life! You must deeply want to enter into this new consciousness. Do not resist expansion into a new mode of operation when you are ready for it, for otherwise you prepare a painful crisis. The less you resist, the smoother the transition into a new, more truthful, more loving state will be.

Commit yourself to go further and deeper in this direction, to help yourself and those around you. Allow this to happen. It is the greatest blessing that can be. You will create the necessary new climate for a new inner environment— inside and out.

You are indeed blessed. Every step of truth, every step toward love, releases more spiritual energy, activates more of your divine nature. *Be* this divine nature!

PART III

Relationship
in the Age of
Expanded Consciousness

The culmination of the relationship between man and woman is in the fusion of the purified personalities on all levels. How do we love, live, and create our relationships in the fullness of the liberated psyche?

The lectures in the last part of this book are given in the context of the significant changes that are taking place at this time in human consciousness. This shift in consciousness is real and a vast number of people are tuned into it all over the world. As we read these particular lectures, we come to understand the manifestations of the man-woman relationship, sexuality, and marriage throughout history as phases in the development of consciousness. It is a fascinating overview. The spiritual meaning of history bridges past, present, and future.

How do we participate, as individual women and men, in this cosmic venture? As we follow the guidance, our own consciousness is being raised, step by step. We can envisage our personal purification process to lead us to the grounded spirituality that the Pathwork is.

The highest definition given by the Guide of the completely self-realized person is one who has reached Christ-consciousness. His definition of the "Christ-consciousness," or the "Christed being" goes way beyond any religious connotation in the old sense. Christ, in the esoteric interpretation, as the man who is also God, represents the accomplishment of the purpose of the human pilgrimage: full selfhood, complete freedom of choice, the incorporation of the divine creative principle, perfect love, and infinite compassion. According to the Guide, though the road is long, to reach its end is possible and even fated for all of us.

The perfect being, who we potentially all are, has integrated all aspects of the undistorted masculine and feminine energies and as such is no longer divided. If you have seen the face of Jesus on Leonardo da Vinci's *Last Supper,* you will remember that it is androgynous: the Christed person has both power and softness. In a drawing of Frederick Franck, I recently saw the face of the risen Christ as being identical with the face of the Buddha—also neither male nor female, but both. The poignancy of the picture was awesome.

Yet, while the Guide teaches us to reach for the ultimate, he gives his full blessing to each one of us as we are now, flawed and also beautiful, and encourages us to live fully in the present, and in our bodies. Fulfillment, happiness is ours, if we so choose, in every moment of our consciously lived lives.

J.S.

Fusion: The Spiritual Significance of Sexuality

Greetings and blessings for every one of you.

Any human manifestation, whether it is natural, instinctual, or man-made, has a deep spiritual significance. All human experience is always symbolic of a wider, deeper, and fuller reality. This lecture will deal with the spiritual meaning of sexuality. *Using the term "sexuality" to represent the total creative force, I will explain how its purpose and spiritual meaning manifests in the human realm.*

How sexuality manifests varies according to the development of each human being. The principle of sexuality manifests differently in the totally self-realized individual, in the average person, and in those who are perhaps still on such a very low level of spiritual development that they are severely blocked and split.

The sexual force is an expression of *consciousness reaching for fusion*. And fusion, which you can also call integration, unification, or oneness is the purpose of Creation. Whatever term we use, the final aim of all split-off beings is to reunify the individualized, separated aspects of the greater consciousness with the whole. The split-off aspects are integrally connected to a great force that motivates individuals to strive toward unification. The pull of this force is irresistible: it exists in all organisms—even in inanimate ones, where human intelligence and perception cannot yet observe it.

The power of sexuality in its most ideal form can convey more fully than any other human experience what spiritual bliss, oneness, and timelessness are. *In the total sexual experience you break through the confines of time and separateness to which your limited mind has bound you.* Such an experience reminds you of your true existence in the eternal.

The blissful experience of fusion and the sense of timelessness in the sexual union depend on the inner unification of the individuals in question, and therefore on their attitudes on all levels of their being. If the sexual experience is an expression of the physical, emotional, mental and spiritual levels, and if these levels are unified with each other without any conflict, then the people who express their being on all these levels in accordance with spiritual law have a sexual experience as complete, fulfilling, rich, joyous, nourishing, sustaining, furthering and reminiscent of spiritual reality as any human experience can be. Then in that blissful experience of total union the fulfillment transcends personal satisfaction and enrichment. These individuals are then also fulfilling a task in the universe. This may seem strange, for the human brain is used to equating task and fulfillment with something arduous, difficult, or even unpleasant. But, in truth, the more complete their joy, pleasure, bliss, and ecstasy, the more creative power do they add to the universal reservoir. Every such experience is like a new star lighting up somewhere in Creation and becoming yet another torch in the darkness of the void that is destined to be filled with light.

Physical, Emotional, Mental, and Spiritual Fusion

What is the meaning of the sexual experience on the physical level? What does the urge to physically unite with another signify? The usual answers, such as the perpetuation of the race or the need for pleasure, are only partial answers and rather superficial at that. *When two human beings are attracted to each other, we might say that they yearn to know each other, to reveal themselves to each other, to let themselves be known and found, and to find the true being of the other person.* By revealing yourself to another being, your own true being can enter the full dimension of that other person's self who is also seeking to know you. This mutual desire which is energized by an involuntary force creates an electrifyingly blissful feeling and longing.

If attraction exists on the physical level, without other levels entering into the expression at least to some degree, the ensuing experience will be disappointing. It can never be more than an infinitesimal and superficial representation of what the soul really longs for—but is too blind to understand and to pursue. Pursuing full union with another soul requires a purification and unification process such as your pathwork.

Since the limited and blind human consciousness merely gropes in the dark, very often your attraction to another person is not directed to the actual person, but rather to an image fabricated in your mind of what the other person should be in order to fulfill your real or imagined needs. The real person in this case is often totally ignored and willfully denied. The desiring person insists on his or her illusion and is angry when the illusion cannot be made to come true. Usually this is mutual—both parties seek someone else, as it were, and do not know it. The measure of fulfillment you experience is a good gauge of how much you seek the real person. The absence of bliss indicates the illusory nature of the search, it reveals instead the superimposition of another person, such as a parent figure, over the real person. When your attraction to another is truly genuine and arises from a real and healthy foundation, it is directed to that specific person to whom you wish to reveal yourself in a most intimate and real way, and with whom you wish to be as closely connected as possible.

The longing for close connection never ceases in the human soul, but it takes different forms in an infant and in an adult. For an infant, closeness is an entirely passive experience: the child takes in, receives, soaks up nourishment and affection as a simple and merely receptive organism, thus illustrating the universal feminine principle. The mother in this case is the giver, and in that capacity the truly feminine woman expresses her masculine principle. For the adult, closeness can be successfully consummated only when the experience is mutual—when both participants actively reach out, give, sustain, nurture, receive, and take in. This organic self-regulating, spontaneous rhythm cannot be determined by the ego-mind. It is the involuntary expression of a lawful process, so exacting, intricate and meaningful, that conveying it to your human scope of understanding is impossible.

The blocks to true fulfillment exist because the infant within the adult personality still seeks its own mode of fulfillment. It seeks a nurturing parent rather than a very specific other person, and it seeks the merely receptive, in-taking kind of closeness. If the fusion is sought with such motivations it can never take place. Hence, the person who desires such an immature union lives in a treadmill of perpetual frustration which then seems to justify his or her caution, withholding, and negativity. The movement toward closeness is split off and a countermovement is generated which causes a short-circuit. The short-circuit is then experienced as an involuntary block, inhibition, and deadness.

On the emotional level, the movement toward fusion must be expressed in a feeling-exchange. What does feeling-exchange mean in adult, realistic terms? Feeling-exchange, or the emotional level of sexuality, is determined by love in its real sense, with all its many aspects and manifestations. You use the word love very freely, but only too often there is no meaning attached to the word when it is spoken, or, worse, the word love is used as a label behind which very different feelings such as ego-needs and negative aims are hidden. People use each other in the most exploitative way and call this love. But what is the vivid, living experience behind the stereotyped label? The experience of love is primarily an attempt to perceive the multiple reality of the other person. *Such an endeavor requires that you temporarily put aside your ego, your own needs, expectations, and personal preoccupations to make yourself empty. Then you can let in what is, let in the other person so you can truly perceive, experience, and feel all the complexities of this other being.* What more fascinating experience could there be?

When you have no stake in maintaining an illusory image of who the other person ought to be, and then resenting it when he or she is not that, you will be open and sufficiently empty to let in what is. This is one way of expressing love. From that solid basis a feeling-exchange can be built.

If you perceive his or her reality, you are free enough of your selfwill, pride, and fear to deal with what is. You will be able to handle even pain and frustration if necessary, so that reality which is ultimately bliss can come to you. The ability to take frustration and pain is essential to giving and receiving and experiencing bliss. On the other hand, if you are very threatened by and defended against pain—the pain of not having your way, the pain of being hurt a little, the pain of having to give up an imaginary or even a real advantage—you will create a hard wall out of your flowing energy stream. Nothing can come into you through this wall, nor can anything flow out from you toward others. You are isolated in the self-created prison of your defense against pain and unpleasantness. You become numb and cannot live fully. You cannot fuse and thus you can have no real pleasure.

Loving, and therefore the ability to give and receive, depends on one's ability to perceive reality with uncluttered vision. This ability, in turn, depends on how well you can suffer pain in an undefended way that is free from manipulative interpretations of the pain. Such interpretations only aim to annul the pain, whereas letting the pain be will make room for a truthful interpretation of the events which bring the pain about.

The aspect of real love which I refer to as letting the other be means more than just accepting where and who the other person is at any given moment. *It means having a vision of the total person, including his or her as yet unrealized potential.* Such a vision of the unmanifest in another person is a great act of love. It has nothing to do with the illusion of manufacturing another kind of person for the purpose of selfwilled needs. If you can give that freedom "to be who you are" to the person you love, you can exchange trust. You thus gain the freedom to assert your own right to be, which you can then do without defiance and without playing your negative games. Positive self-assertion stems from the guilt-free state that follows the truly giving attitude. If you can say "yes" to wholeheartedly giving, you can also say "no." If you truly give, you can also assert your inner right to receive—and that is not to be confused with childish, neurotic demands.

Not giving feelings makes mutual exchange impossible. Since in reality giving and receiving are one, you cannot give to others without also giving to yourself. Conversely, by withholding from others, you inevitably withhold from yourself. You then blame the consequent deprivation on the other person because you are still clinging to the illusion that giving and receiving are two separate acts. The fusion you long for can only come about if every feeling you long to receive, every single aspect of loving, is richly flowing out of you. These aspects of love include tenderness, warmth, respect, and also the recognition of the essence of the other with his or her capacity for growth, change, and goodness. Add to these patience, and giving the other the benefit of the doubt. Make room for alternative interpretations. Trust, and give the other room to unfold and to be. You also yearn passionately to be given these aspects of perfect love. Fusion can take place on the emotional level only when you are fully committed to learn to expand your own capacity to give these components of perfect love.

But in order to fuse emotionally—and therefore totally—it is equally necessary to express yourself truthfully toward the other person, even when this may not be welcome or desired. Not doing so under the guise of a so-called loving goodness and taking it in silence is sentimental and usually dishonest. For in reality you merely fear the unpleasant consequences and are thus not willing to risk pain, exposure, confrontation, and the hard work of reintegrating the relationship on both a higher and more profound level. This can only be done healthily without guilt when you have dealt with and eliminated your own cruelty. As long as any cruelty exists in you, you will never be able to tell the truth to others without hurting them, because the hidden motive to hurt others so pervades your energies and affects your actions and words that it paralyzes your courage to speak up and confront a situation that requires improvement.

How then can an unhampered giving of love be reinstituted and increased? It is possible that you are free from cruelty and can speak up in a totally constructive way, and still the other person is hurt—maybe because he or she insists on never being criticized or frustrated. But if you can deal with the hurt that arises in you from this reaction, you can truly risk this event and battle it through so that an open exchange of feelings can be made possible. You will find that the more you act out of your sincere intention to love and feel more deeply, the more fruitful the outcome will be when you risk offending your partner. Conversely, when you "speak the truth" because you need to hurt but do not wish to admit it, the outcome must be undesirable. Your guilt for this hidden motivation will be a shield standing between you and the truth and between you and the other person.

The fulfillment and bliss your soul longs for can only be satisfied through fusion with another consciousness. It depends on your ability to risk, to confront, to admit your most guarded secret, and as a result to speak up when the other person puts obstructions in the way. You must also recognize your own reluctance to express your best feelings when the unexpressed negativities and hidden games of your partner make this impossible. The positive assertion I speak of here is entirely different from making a blaming demand, which in fact puts the responsibility on the other person. The right kind of assertion does not blame the other, and yet it also recognizes what the other is doing. When you no longer have a stake in blaming, you can truly speak up. When your recognition of your partner's negative contribution stems from the clear vision you could only gain as a result of self-confrontation and deep honesty, then you will risk, and the temporary pain will not diminish you.

In order to fuse emotionally, honest exchange at the risk of occasional crises is necessary. Honest exchange is totally dependent on the individuals' self-honesty and goodwill to abandon dishonest, hurtful, and destructive patterns. If you are inhibited and afraid, you also inhibit the mutual scope and depth of the bliss that arises from fusion. In that case, you have to ask yourselves where this fear has its origin in both of you. And since you can only be responsible for yourself, ask especially where the fear originates in you. Where is the cruelty in you that makes you afraid of saying what you see? Where does your blindness toward yourself inevitably blind you toward the other person, so that you are unsure and defensive about what you see—and consequently militant and hostile. Again, emotional fusion can exist only to the degree that the prerequisites I discussed here are fulfilled.

Mental fusion exists on the level of the thinking mind. The ability to exchange the deepest ideas and thoughts and to risk disagreement and disapproval are basic. Mental fusion can only exist when there is a certain blend of compatibility. Two compatible partners have to share certain fundamental ideas about life. They must also be spiritually more or less on the same plane of development. This does not mean that every small idea must be shared. That is quite impossible and divergence in some ways is necessary. It is both a result of the variety within human beings and also a necessary help for each one's further development.

Several qualities are required for reaching mental fusion. One is the need to grow toward truthful understanding of each other, another is the humility to search for, and discard if necessary, the ideas and opinions you both may hold. You also need the humility to let the other and also yourself be right or wrong. The very act of looking for a deeper way of truth concerning even the tiniest issues provides wonderful fuel for growth and helps you to reach deeper union on the mental level. The attitudes you bring to bear on the points of difference and the ways you approach them are important. Do you avoid any confrontation of ideas because it is simply too uncomfortable to make waves? Do you agree superficially so as to have peace because the issue is "unimportant" anyway? Can you perhaps not be bothered to even deeply think about things that do not directly concern you? Or do you insist on being "right" merely for its own sake? Is disagreement a way to find an outlet for the negative feelings and thoughts stored up in you which you do not choose to deal with constructively?

The freedom to have different ideas can be granted only when you are both anchored in spiritual truth. When spiritual reality is forever the ultimate aim, you also know that there is only one truth. And this applies every bit as much to the large vital issues as to the smallest everyday inanities. But you also know that this one truth has many facets, often including two apparent opposites that are parts of one whole. With spiritual truth as the ultimate goal, you will sit lightly in the saddle of opinions, ideas, and thoughts. This will make it possible to share and exchange them. If you always aim for the inner truth, the spiritual truth, then the little disagreements or different opinions slowly disappear. First they cease to matter; then they become integrated or fused in the all-uniting truth of spirit.

Mental sharing must not be neglected. One often sees relationships with sexual sharing and, to a degree, emotional sharing, but mental sharing is strangely neglected in a world that stresses the importance of the intellect, ideas, and the mind so much. Yet people live next to each other day in and day out, depriving themselves and each other of the joys of mental fusion. They do not mentally expose their innermost beings, ideas, beliefs, dreams, aspirations, feelings, fears, goals, yearnings, insecurities, and hopes. The world of the mind and ideas is an integral part of total sharing. And it is quite impossible for one person to fuse with another on one level in a truly satisfying way, while keeping separate on any of the other levels and thus not staying in tune with the natural movement toward fusion. For instance, quite often when frustration is ascribed to sexual incompatibility, the sexual incompatibility may not be a result of an absence of physical attraction at all. It may be the result of insufficient fusion on any one or all of the other levels.

Spiritual fusion is always a natural result of fusion on the physical, emotional, and mental levels. Fusion existing on these three levels means that the parties involved must be highly developed spiritual beings, actively working on and involved in a spiritual path. They must be sufficiently awake to consciously and deliberately seek spiritual truth. Reaching the spiritual self must be one's primary aim if total fusion is to exist. It is therefore true that the fulfillment and bliss that every created being longs for is possible to the degree that a person's spiritual development has advanced and still continues to advance. Such a state is maintained to the degree that the partners are in movement, and to the degree that destructiveness has made room for constructive, outgoing, positive attitudes and behavior. All too often human beings are stuck and have no intention of moving out of their stagnation. They are then surprised when their yearning for oneness remains unfulfilled, and they blame others, circumstances, and life for it.

All matters of life must finally be related to the spiritual self and to spiritual reality. All disputes can truly be resolved and conciliated only in the spiritual self, which is one in all created beings. When two human beings fuse with the awareness that there is a spiritual world within both of them where they can discover their oneness, then spiritual union takes place. The tremendous creative power of the sexual force generated through union on all levels has self-perpetuating life with both positive and negative aspects. Participating in this life, the partners striving for union set something in motion that takes on its own momentum like a stream which the human personality has to learn to follow.

A Person's Sexuality Mirrors the Problems of the Soul

Whatever exists within the human psyche shows up in the sexual experience; it is impossible to keep anything out. The actual form of the sexual experience is therefore an infallible indicator of where a person's psyche is. It will reveal where a person is liberated and at one with divine law, where evil and destructive, and where stuck and stagnant because the destructiveness is hidden and not dealt with. Hidden facets become magnetized and energized by the sexual current, thereby determining its direction. When this direction is negative and therefore shamefully denied, both the person's development and the vitality of the life force are hindered.

The powerful creative energy inherent in sexual expression creates a condition where all character attitudes and all aspects of one's most hidden nature must manifest. Unfortunately, human beings are extremely blind to this. Even the most advanced psychology is oblivious to the fact that the way in which sexuality manifests—not necessarily in action, but in inclination—reveals one's whole character with all one's attitudes, personality and ego trends, problems and impurities, as well as one's already purified beauty. All that information is revealed and is available to anyone who knows how and where to look for it.

All too often sexual attitudes are dealt with in a glib way by simply judging them as healthy or neurotic, or morally right or wrong. People also defiantly refuse to recognize the clues contained in them. In such cases these clues are separated from the rest of the person as if such inclinations were purely a matter of taste, or inborn traits such as being born with blue eyes or brown. Labels are so often supposed to take care of the matter. Often the spiritual message of the inner reality is completely overlooked, no matter how clearly and loudly it speaks through a person's sexual inclinations, whether allowed to manifest, or denied and repressed. If character defects deform one's sexual drive into cruel, destructive fantasies, to act them out is just as unnecessary as to act out other destructive feelings. The same is true for any murderous feelings you own up to in your pathwork; they don't need to be acted out in order for you to be able to face, understand, accept, and deal with them and to recognize their inner meaning.

It is precisely because sexual energy is so powerful that every small, apparently insignificant attitude existing in the human personality reappears symbolically in one's sexual expression. The way sexuality expresses itself in an individual mirrors those inner aspects which the person desperately needs to be aware of. My friends, for you it is a question of learning to use this knowledge. Look at your sexuality in a new way. What does it reveal to you about your non-sexual nature, about your person, your attitudes, and so on? Where does your sexuality bring out your problems, and where and how does it reveal your purified nature?

When you and your partner are not fusing at one of the four levels, then that must be apparent in your life. Let us say that your attractions, needs, and desires are strong on the physical level. Let us assume you are ready to expose yourself on that level and seek fusion there. But let us also assume that on the emotional and/or mental level this is not at all the case. There you wish to keep separate and do not wish either to give, or to risk, or to constantly integrate each level on a yet higher plane. The physical level will then not only become severely restricted, but the nature of your sexual drive must, in one form or another, reveal the emotional and mental attitudes you may keep hidden. You may have no notion that these attitudes reappear in a sexualized form, infused and magnetized by the sexual force.

If the negativities of the psychic system are not allowed into consciousness, the sexual experience must be blocked, flat, unsatisfactory, mechanical and, in more severe cases, even totally paralyzed. If the denial is removed, the sexual inclination may show up character tendencies such as finding pleasure in being cruel. There are many variations and details that cannot possibly be generalized. For example, if both the guilt and the ensuing self-punishment are denied and repressed, they may show up in a sexual inclination to be hurt, humiliated, or rejected. There are innumerable possibilities and meanings. Each sexual fantasy must be reawakened and allowed to be, so that it can be understood. This is the only way to bring stagnant sexual energy back into a flowing state, even if it first means living out the fantasies, either in your mind or in a playful way within an intimate and established relationship.

Often the deviant sexual expression is quite conscious and indulged in and enjoyed to whatever degree it is possible to do so in such a hampered way. However, the sexual expression is not connected to its deeper meaning—the person simply assumes, "this is the way I am," and is unwilling to give up the pleasure, convinced that this is the only way he or she can have pleasure. Such a conviction is totally untrue; the pleasure that would become available if the negative characteristic were recognized is incomparably higher in intensity and quality, and nothing has to be given up for it. In order to change, one first allows oneself to make the connections between the recognized negative trait and the non-sexual aspects of one's being. From there, a natural transformation in the direction of the sexual current will organically develop.

You who have been working on this path for some time have already confronted some of your negativities. Can you imagine that these negativities do not express themselves in your sexuality? Can you, even for an instant, assume that your negativities do not manifest in your sexual attitudes and therefore do not influence your capacity for fulfillment, fusion, and bliss? To believe that would indeed be foolish. So look for what specific negativities cause what specific manifestations in you. This will be an extremely exciting undertaking for you, one that will yield many keys. The more specific you can be, the more revealing and enlivening your insights and your understanding about yourself will be.

You all know that making the connections between cause and effect is an important aspect of self-confrontation and personal development. The greatest pain and dissonance in the human personality is caused by the disconnection between cause and effect. Nothing is more painful than suffering an effect whose cause you ignore.

Are Spirituality and Sexuality in Conflict?

For most human beings it is still inconceivable to *combine sexuality with spirituality*. This is bound to change soon; the spiritual influxes of today have already wrought the beginning of a new era. In former times, sexuality and spirituality were considered antithetical. It was not known that true spiritual union is a consummate result of union on all levels of being, including the physical-sexual one. It was not known that total integration and oneness must bring sexuality into alignment with spirituality. The realization of your spiritual life is possible only as a result of total unification on all these other levels, and certainly never as a result of splitting off any one part from the other. The real meaning of spirituality is oneness and wholeness, and that means it must include all there is. Satisfying relationships therefore always mirror the degree of the individual's inner unification. If you cannot find union with others, then you are in disunity within yourself.

The difficulty human beings have in unifying spirituality and sexuality, even as concepts, is due precisely to what I explained before—namely, the fact that hidden evil manifests in and through the sexual expression. This is why for centuries spiritual teachings have postulated that sexuality is a hindrance to spiritual development. At an earlier time in history, there was a reason for such postulates. They were not all that wrong at that time. Early humanity's less developed state made people act out their brutality and bestiality through their sexuality. Consciousness and conscience, the influx of the spirit, existed to a much lesser degree then. Everything was acted out with impunity and in self-righteousness. The stronger ones had the rights and needed no excuses. The ability to practice restraint and discipline was practically non-existent. The capacity for empathy with others was extremely weak and rare. In such a world the powerful drives had to be restrained in order to make any influx of the spirit possible. This explains the long eras when spiritual exercises were used to restrain natural instincts. On the one hand, spiritual development proceeded, on the other it also constrained humanity's natural drives, and this was temporarily necessary.

Only now, as humanity enters a new spiritual era of unfoldment, are human beings strong enough to look at their hidden instincts and to purify them without the danger of acting them out. Yet, even today hardly anyone knows the fine line between safe, honest expression and admission of negative material, and destructive acting out. You on this path are indeed pioneers in learning the all-important art of making the distinction. Only in this way can you unify your total person, purify all aspects of yourself, and safely bring out the sexual drive in whatever way it now manifests. The current predominance of stagnation, low vitality, and frequent sexual problems are a result of hemming in your negative life force because you have not been able to deal with it safely. You are now learning a new and marvelous method of freeing your instincts for the purpose of purifying and revitalizing your life.

If the energy of the life force is concentrated in unrecognized and unfaced evil, then the energy itself is feared, and a state of stagnation becomes preferred as the lesser evil. This numbness is also painful and the sexual yearning may become unbearable, but the inner person is still too puzzled and fearful to face the truth. The evil is denied, and the personality may then try to force the sexual drive artificially with very unsatisfactory results. The person may resort to artificial stimulants, and then sexuality becomes even more split off from the rest of the personality.

The splits among the levels creates further short-circuits. They may manifest in the following ways: The emotional level expresses, "I do not want to love" which indicates denied hate. The mental level might say, "I ought to love, and if I do not, I am bad and have no pleasure. So I must force myself to love." Another mental level may simultaneously say, "I have no use for you; you are bad," as an excuse and explanation for not loving. The physical-sexual level may say, "I want to possess you to have my pleasure." In such a predicament, sexuality is either annulled, or it functions in what is referred to as a perversion—pleasure in giving pain, pleasure in denying the self and the other. Hating, selfish, cruel sex always produces guilt. The guilt feelings are then rationalized and dismissed as coming from a puritanical and unenlightened judgmental attitude. But guilt still prevails, in spite of all "enlightenment."

The Origins of Sexual Guilt

What is the origin of such a guilt? Surely one feels true guilt for the concealed hatred and brutality that manifest covertly in sexual expressions, whether or not one admits having them. If one's desire to put down others, to be self-serving, or to be exploitative and unmindful of others are not dealt with directly, they pollute holy sexuality. And *sexuality is indeed holy.* When sexuality is used in the service of ego aggrandizement and lust for power, it cannot help but produce guilt—guilt that is "inexplicable" or explained away by referring to people's backgrounds and early influences.

Nothing is as dangerous as using a powerful spiritual energy in a destructive, inverted way, whether in actual fact or in thought and attitude only. When killing and hating are embedded in sexuality, sexuality becomes vicious and antagonistic to spirituality. People acted out for millennia the most bestial drives in sexuality, thus giving rise to the belief that sexuality was in itself bestial. Only now is it possible for human beings to take every conceivable evil, face it, and not act upon it. Today there is a conscience in people that makes them quite aware when they are vicious. The awareness is not always on the surface, but it nevertheless exists within the psyche. Therefore there is a reluctance to give in to the sexual drive, for it can bring out one's denied negativities, one's evil, and destructiveness.

If you use this key in the spirit of the pathwork, to allow yourself to see and admit the truth, you will not only gain deeper insight into yourself, make new connections, and purify yourself more, but you will also activate your sexual power that was so elusive before. You will free your sexuality and simultaneously integrate it with your spiritual self—without an untimely, compulsive forcing, but in a natural process. You thus will free the sexual energy from the negative involvement. Deal with this, my friends. The more you do this, the less blocked you will find yourself to be. The more spontaneous the inner movement will become, the more revitalized you will be through the experience of fusion, and the better your involuntary processes will function. *Your most secret sexual fantasies, if examined in the light of clear truth for what they really are, will be your liberation.* No truth is ever too much to bear. No truth, if perceived with a sense of realism, can ever diminish your spirit and your true self. Thus you become alive and awaken from your deadness. You will free yourself from your fears.

Before ending this lecture, I want to recapitulate just one more teaching in connection with this topic, to make a connection.

The masculine and feminine principles in the universe express themselves in every creative act. How do they express themselves between and within the two partners? The masculine principle expresses the outgoing movement of reaching, giving, acting, initiating, asserting. The feminine principle expresses the receptive movement of taking in and nurturing. In distortion and negativity the masculine principle manifests as hostile aggression, hitting rather than giving and reaching. The feminine principle in distortion turns from loving receptivity and nurturing to grasping, grabbing, stealing, holding tight, catching, and taking without letting go. These principles manifest in every living act. Both principles, in harmony and distortion, exist in both men and women. They can easily be detected with a minimum of self-observation. They are manifest as soul movements that may or may not also manifest as physical acts.

Total Fusion

These movements exist in absolutely everything that could ever be created or could ever be. They are integral manifestations of Creation. Once you ascertain the manner in which both principles express themselves in you, it is easily possible to connect these expressions with your mental, emotional, and physical levels. Allow yourself this vision. Satisfying fusion between a man and a woman is possible only to the degree that both principles work in harmony within both partners, and thus complement each other in the act of fusion. If there is no harmonious interplay within your own psychic system of the masculine and feminine principles, if there is distortion and imbalance there, then this must inevitably also manifest in your choice of partner and in the way you conduct the relationship.

Harmonious merging builds up to a point of total fusion. Total fusion is the fulfillment which the two movements find in their culmination. The point of fusion which you may call orgasm in the unifying of two loving mates is the total fulfillment; the aim has been accomplished in spirit to the degree that the fusion is now possible for the striving entities—in whatever creative act. You can have this creative experience only to the degree that you abandon negativities and egotistical defenses and welcome the spontaneous, involuntary movement toward union that issues forth from your innermost being. The creative experience will continue to expand until total union with the whole takes place. Then the entity stays at the point of fusion in unending spiritual bliss. But as long as the universe has not found its completion by filling the void with spiritual light, orgasm in creation can only be temporary. Hence the parts find themselves separate again and continue their striving forever more, until one is all and all is one, until there is no more darkness and only spiritual light, truth, and beauty prevail.

If all of you could deeply know that you have an inexhaustible treasure of security, love, and light in you! The only thing that blocks you off from it is your thinking, your not knowing, your not wanting to feel, to know, and to consider this truth. Make use of this truth.

I leave you with a golden flow of energy. Be blessed in the truth of life that is available at all times, in the truth of love, in the love of truth, and in the peace of spiritual reality.

CHAPTER 14

The New Woman and the New Man

Greetings, my very beloved, dearest friends. Blessings for every one of you here. Tonight I shall speak of the evolution of consciousness as it relates to women and to the man-woman relationship. One cannot discuss this topic without noting the evolving relationship between the sexes.

As the planet is maturing, so are men and women. What does this really mean? *How have woman and man evolved and where are they going?* What is the ultimate realization of womanhood—and of manhood? Woman is coming into her own in this phase of history; she is coming out of her confinement.

A Historical Overview

At the dawn of history, people distrusted anything that was or seemed different, strange, foreign. Distrust of the opposite sex was also very strong. Man innately distrusted woman, and woman, man. Each seemed justified in his or her distrust because of the other's distrustful attitude. Since man was physically stronger, and since physicality was the sole expression of early humans, man also assumed a general aura of superiority over all who were weaker.

The mutual distrust and man's physical domination was very overtly acted out in these early periods of humanity. Since then the same traits and attitudes have remained embedded in the consciousness of woman and man, though to a lesser degree.

Today they may be overshadowed by more realistic and mature awareness; they may not be acted out in the same way, but a dark corner in the psyche remains that needs to be exposed to consciousness and changed.

When you look back in history, you can see that the entire species did what so many individuals do: it retained an attitude long after it made sense. Man retained his superiority long after physical prowess ceased to be the prime value. Other values that apply equally to both sexes emerged as development progressed. Yet men—and often women as well—persisted in considering man superior and woman inferior, and even intellectually and morally weaker than man. But you all know this.

To the degree man did not deal with his own feelings of inferiority and weakness, and wished to pretend that he did not have these feelings, he assumed a position of arrogance and superiority over those who were physically weaker. He needed slaves in order to convince himself of his own value. This applied to animals, to peoples whom he subjugated through warfare, and also to women. Woman assumed a mental and emotional position of dependency, thus actively participating in her enslavement.

Man feared those who were physically stronger than he. The more he feared them, the greater his urge became to subjugate weaker people. This human trait in the unenlightened person, which you well know from your own inner processes, is compensation. It still exists in human consciousness. It is not something that woman is free of either. When you look very deeply into your own consciousness, you will find similar attitudes.

Why has woman been subjugated and denied her birthright of self-expression, of mental, emotional, and spiritual equality with man so long after physical prowess has ceased to be an individual's main value? Woman could not simply be a victim of man's egotistical desire to feel superior and stronger and to possess her as an object. What was her contribution to this situation?

You, my friends on this path, no longer find it difficult to ascertain where you do not want to assume self-responsibility, where you want to be taken care of by a stronger authority figure. Likewise, in the old relationships between man and woman, the woman victimized herself by a denial of self-responsibility; she chose the line of least resistance so she could be taken care of. She wanted an authority figure to make decisions for her and battle with the hardships of life. She wanted to indulge in the pseudo-comfort of dependency.

This has turned out to be a disappointing, unfulfilling way of life for her. All misconceptions sooner or later turn out this way. But woman still abstains from taking her share of responsibility. She still puts all the blame on man.

The new women's movement contains a great deal of truth, but it is, like all dualistic approaches, a half-truth. The full truth is that woman indeed possesses the same faculties of intelligence, resourcefulness, creativity, psychic strength, and productive self-expression as man. To claim that she does not, makes no sense at all and has become a game on the part of man, who does not want to face his own feelings of weakness and inferiority and who therefore needs to feel superior to woman.

By the same token, woman, in order to make the new women's movement truly meaningful, must ascertain within herself the part that has invited her enslavement. I would venture to say that the stronger the rebellion and the blaming of the opposite sex, the stronger must also be, within the soul of that individual woman, the desire not to govern her own life, not to be responsible, but to lean on someone else. To the degree she makes unfair and unrealizable demands, she must resent and blame male authority and play the victim game.

Similarly, to the degree man does not face his fears, guilts, and weaknesses, he will play a power game in one form or another and then resent the woman for exploiting him and overburdening him. The immature soul of both wants the advantage without paying the price: man wants the superior position but resents the price of taking care of a parasite.

Woman wants the advantage of being taken care of, but resents the price of losing her autonomy. Both play the same game but hesitate to see how they mutually create this distortion.

What is Underneath the Stereotypes?

On a still deeper level of consciousness, one finds the opposite of the manifest behavior. The man also shrinks from the responsibility of adulthood and envies the woman her socially sanctioned position. He compensates for this by overemphasizing the power game. The woman hides the part in her where she, too, wants to be aggressive, powerful, strong—not only in the real, but also in the distorted sense. She envies man's superior position. In earlier times, this side of her had to be totally repressed. It was as socially unacceptable as the man's hidden wishes. Only recently has this part emerged, but it is still often confused with genuine selfhood.

Both men and women must find their way out of their dualistic confusions. How can they both have emotional fulfillment and be autonomous adults?

When movements, orientations, and philosophies deal not with the whole picture but only with half of it, it is impossible to right the balance. Although in the course of evolution the pendulum must swing from one extreme to its exact opposite, a deeper insight can help one to avoid excess.

You already know that dualism opposes the unitive consciousness. In duality, man will feel superior and believe woman to be inferior. He will consequently exploit her but will also feel exploited by her. In such a relationship fulfillment is impossible. The woman will feel that she is being unfairly exploited by the physically stronger man and will blame him for victimizing her. Both will fail to see the other side, where they are indeed very similar and where they complement one another in a distorted way.

Both the feminine and the masculine principles must be represented in the healthy individual. They may not be expressed in exactly the same way in man as in woman, since the differences make a complementary whole. But the differences are not qualitative; they must never lead to a judgment that one is better or more developed than the other.

The Fully Autonomous Woman

Let me paint a picture of the woman in the age of expanded consciousness and then apply it to the relationship between the sexes. The new woman is completely self-responsible and therefore free. She stands on her own two feet, not only materially, but also intellectually, mentally, and emotionally. By that I mean specifically that she knows that no man can give her happiness and flowing feelings unless she herself produces them through loving and through integrity, through opening her heart to loving and her mind to her own inner truth. The new woman knows that loving a man and surrendering to her feelings for the man enhances her strength. There is no conflict for the new woman between being a productive, creative, contributing member of society and being a loving mate. In fact, real love is not possible for someone to whom one plays a slave in order to avoid self-responsibility. The old fairy tale that a woman's career will make her less of a woman, less feelingful, less loving, less equipped to be a giving mate, has never had any substance.

The new state requires a strength and autonomy that has to be earned. It needs to be earned by shouldering the weight of reality, with all it entails, but not in a spirit of hate, rebellion, competition, defiance, not by imitating the worst excesses and distortions of manhood, the negative aggression and the power games. It has to be done through the power of truth and love, from the higher self. Whenever something real is denied because of the misconceptions that it is too difficult, those difficulties must first be accepted. They will then prove not so difficult at all. Self-responsibility seems difficult, but is not once the apparent hardships are accepted, because such acceptance amounts to an honest approach to life.

Where distortion still exists, woman still wants from the man what she refuses to give to herself. For the new woman this will not be the case. This does not mean that two people sharing their life do not also share, naturally, their difficulties. But I am not talking about that here. You know perfectly well from your pathwork that what you secretly wanted from a superior father authority you have shifted onto a mate. You also know how such an implicit desire is bound to destroy any relationship. It is bound to make you resent and fear the very authority you wish to exploit. Love can flower only in a climate of true equality, where no fear exists and therefore neither defense nor blame. Contrary to the fairy tale that femininity blossoms when the woman is just a servant to the man, feelings can actually blossom only when the woman is free, autonomous, independent in the best sense of the word. Fulfillment is completely dependent on a true state of equality. The moment one feels superior to the other, one's respect is lowered and the feelings close. The moment one feels inferior to the other, resentment, fear, envy become inescapable, and that, too, closes the heart.

The new woman is neither a slave to the man, nor is she his competitor. Therefore she can love, and her love will not lessen her creative self-expression but rather enhance it, just as her creative contribution to life will enhance her capacity to love. That is the new woman.

The Fully Autonomous Man

The man in the age of expanded consciousness will no longer need a weaker mate in order to deny his own weakness. He meets his own weakness, faces it, and thereby gains his real strength. He realizes that his weakness always comes from guilt, and his self-rejection is always a denial of the integrity of his higher self in one form or another. Therefore the need for a slave no longer exists in him. The man is then not threatened by an equal. He does not require an inferior mate to convince himself of his acceptability, which, of course, is then anyway illusory. Once he faces his weakness he must gain his true strength. Therefore his relationship to the woman is truly one of equality; he is not threatened by someone who is as creative, as adequate, as morally strong, as intelligent as himself. He will not need to play the master. Again, this enables man to open his heart and to experience a fulfillment that was previously quite impossible.

Whatever vicious circles used to confine him will now turn into benign circles. Instead of inferiority feelings closing the heart, creating resentment, hate, and therefore frustration and blame of the other sex, the benign circle will open the heart. The fully autonomous, self-responsible, self-actualizing man and woman have nothing to fear, to envy, to resent in the other sex. Therefore they can open all the channels of feelings and experience fulfillment as well as a sense of gratitude toward the mate. Thus two equals help each other in their growth as individuals, as man and woman. This is the new man, the new woman, and the new relationship.

Where this does not yet exist, the mere fact that you can point out the fallacies, distorted expectations, illusory aims and negative feelings within you and can recognize your stake in maintaining an inner warfare, will give you an entirely different stand toward yourself and the other. So the new man and the new woman are not necessarily perfect and totally developed individuals. Rather, they are individuals who look for the reasons of their lack of fulfillment just as much in themselves as in the other. Thus they can recognize a negative mutuality that needs to be worked on together. They do not widen the gap with self-righteous blaming between the self and the other, between the self and truth.

Autonomy, in an ever-growing process, dissolves distrust. The distrust that still exists between the sexes is a residue of ancient times. In the age which we are now entering, differences will no longer induce fear. When the universe is trusted, difference always possesses a special attraction. When you do not fear difference but are attracted by it, you fully actualize yourself and dissolve blocks of untruth. Thus you realize your highest potentials. Use this recognition as a gauge of your intent to remain in untruth and suffering or not.

At present, humanity's consciousness encompasses all the stages in the development of the man-woman relationship. You, personally, may consciously embrace the highest ideals. But on deeper levels, your emotional reactions may not at all agree with the ideas you consciously hold. It is important to see where and how you deviate from them. For that is the only way to safeguard against imbalance within—and thus against creating disharmony externally.

There is of course one key to everything, and that key is love. Without love nothing could be mended, nothing could unify, no truth could ever be gained. And yet it is equally true that love cannot be won without truth. In a deep corner of your hearts, hate and fear, resentment and distrust of the opposite sex still prevail. Even more importantly, the will to maintain this state, the intention to perpetuate and hide these feelings, prevent the flowering of the hearts and minds of both men and women. To the degree that you still cling to the old state, you have not gained your own self and are not able to relate well to the other sex and fulfill yourself. Seeking fulfillment with the old attitude unchanged is utterly futile.

So, I say to you, my dearest friends, find that corner in your heart, that small hidden crevice where you hate the opposite sex. You may defend against recognizing this by blaming, accusing, resenting, and closing your heart with apparent justification. The woman will use the victim game; the man will use the blame and superiority game. He will blame the woman for exploiting and using him, and will feel superior to that part in her that makes her weak. Temporarily, the pendulum has swung to the opposite extreme. The woman has become militant, often forgetting her heart, her love for the man, rejecting love. In the countermovement of the pendulum, man has left his positive aggression behind and has expressed a weakness he would never have let himself expose in previous eras.

The Present is an Era of Change

All the pendulum swings have a purpose: to find the true centered state. Man will now find his real strength. He had to leave the false strength, the false superiority, behind. He had to become temporarily weak, but is now coming into a new strength because he is able to face his weakness. That is how he expands the real values and the real power in him. Therefore he no longer needs to be the superior member of the team. He can afford to relate from the heart, on the feeling level, to his partner. He can likewise relate intellectually on a level of equality with her. That is the new man.

Therefore, my dearest friends, you need to look into that part of you where you do not want to forgive, to understand the truth, and where you want to preserve your case and go on hating. You need to release the hatred toward the opposite sex. You have to pray for the ability to love, to forgive, to understand, and to see that what you hate, fear, and distrust exists in you in exactly the same way as in the other, though perhaps manifesting differently.

The woman represents the active principle just as much as the man. And the man represents the receptive principle as much as the woman. In their coming together in sexual union this may not always manifest in the same way, but the inner forces must combine both the active and receptive principles, otherwise imbalance exists. No true man can be a man without incorporating the receptive, or feminine, principle. If he expresses only the masculine principle, he becomes a caricature of a man. He is then a bully, a tyrant, an exaggeration, a falsehood. By the same token, a woman who expresses only the receptive principle is a caricature of a woman and is truly an infant who leans on others, who negates her autonomy. So to be fully receptive on the feeling level, woman has to express the active principle every bit as much as man.

The two principles must be represented in both and must complement one another, while they are, at times, also parallel. This perfect balance cannot occur through an intellectual decision. It can be found organically only through the inner act of love, the inner act of releasing the opposite sex from the bondage of hate, distrust, and blame. When this release is pronounced in daily meditation, when God's grace can go to work within the consciousness of the woman as well as of the man, then love will lead to truth, just as truth will lead to love.

Individuals of both sexes will function as equally productive human beings in the new universe, complementing and aiding one another, loving one another, respecting one another, and creating bliss and a new world for each other side by side. This is the way life should be.

Career and Partnership

You may have noticed a pattern on this path, my friends, in which an individual must first resolve career problems in order to resolve partnership problems. In the context of this lecture this will become very clear. When relationships are formed to act out dependency, parasitism, exploitation of the other, and/or the need to dominate and enslave, then, for a while, these individuals have to fend for themselves until a certain minimal autonomy and independence have been established. Once the creative channel is opened up, the new freedom can release previously trapped energies, and people can begin to relate to the opposite sex in an entirely new way.

I was very happy to give you this lecture, for everything that leads toward the further unfoldment of the whole person—both man and woman—is a joyful experience for us in our world. See the beauty of the Christ-consciousness that goes through all of you. Be in peace, be in God.

CHAPTER 15

The New Marriage

Blessed are your lives, all your thoughts, strivings, and endeavors, my dearly beloved friends.

The spiritual forces in the universe are so strong that an unpurified personality cannot bear them. To the degree that both negativity and distortion exist in an individual's mind and consciousness, these powerful currents manifest as crisis, pain, and danger. Yet, to be receptive to the divine influx of the Christ consciousness and to be part of it is the deep longing of every soul.

The development of the institution of marriage is of great significance from this point of view. A deeper insight is needed now so that you can widen and deepen your understanding of marriage and use this knowledge to articulate your longing. This is always the first step toward bringing what you long for into actuality.

Marriage Throughout the Ages

Let us consider the evolution of marriage thus far and open your vision to the future, so that you will view the current attitude toward this institution with the larger picture in mind. History can be properly understood only when the spiritual meaning that underlies earthly events is gleaned.

In the not-too-distant past, marriage served a number of functions, but least of all sharing, love, or mutuality on all levels of the personality. In fact, love, mutual sexual surrender and the profound exchange of dynamic energy levels was rejected and condemned. Marriage was supposed to be a financial and social contract to satisfy other personality functions and lower motives. Financial and social advantages were of primary importance. Even more significant was the absolute conviction that these motives were morally right and virtuous. Men married women who brought a good dowry and who raised man's social image. In other words, greed and pride were glamorized and endowed with righteousness.

Men considered themselves the superiors of women. Marrying a woman meant nothing more than acquiring a slave who obeyed the master of the house; who saw to it that the man received every comfort and convenience but made no demands for herself. In exchange for these services, which included being an object for man's mostly quite impersonal lust, the woman received material security. Her only responsibility was to be an adequate object for her master. Of course you understand, my friends, that man's responsibility entailed much more than mere financial responsibility. Since woman was not considered a full-fledged equal, morally she was barely responsible. In those centuries emotional and mental responsibility did not exist as a concept, but they certainly existed as a fact. Even without the awareness of the concept, men acknowledged this responsibility toward other men but totally neglected it when dealing with women.

Obviously, this was not only the result of man's distortion and negativity; it was just as much the result of a strongly embedded intentionality in the woman's psyche. Women refused self-responsibility on all levels for the longest time and therefore co-created the unequal relationship between the sexes.

Fear of the Power of the Unified Current

Both sexes equally feared—and still fear—the powerful spiritual energies involved in the forces of love, eros, and sexuality between man and woman. This cosmic power is the creative stream itself from which everything is made. This powerful current can express itself in many ways, not just as a binding force between a man and a woman. It can be expressed through spiritual disciplines within an individual, merging the masculine and feminine principles and power currents within an individual soul.

The unpurified soul cannot stand this power current. To the degree unpurified soul substance festers in the personality, the power current has to be denied, suppressed, and split. Sexuality that manifests without love, commitment, and respect is just such a split-off, denied power current. Human beings who believe that pornographic or promiscuous sex is more pleasurable than the sexuality that streams from a unified wholeness and combines with love and spiritual union could not be more wrong. The precise opposite is true. But the power of such sexuality is so strong that it cannot be borne by the soul that still lives partly in darkness.

Another human error is the belief that a married couple faithful to one another is necessarily beyond the stage of split-off sexuality. The typical marriage of former times, which I described earlier, was a complete suppression, repression, and denial of the spiritual power currents. *In the man the denial often still manifests as an inability to experience strong sexual feelings for the woman he loves,* honors, and respects. Sometimes the unconscious fear of the power current is so strong that the split is total, and a man finds himself unable to experience sexuality with a loved woman. In many cases, however, the split exists with one and the same woman. A man can give relative honor and relative love to a woman he has married, yet blot out her reality during the act of sexual union. This act can be performed only when the woman becomes a low object in the man's mind. Pornographic sex can take place within the framework of respectable marriage and is socially fully accepted.

For the woman, the denial of the unified power current often manifested in total denial of the sexual reality of her body. Whenever her sexuality manifested in spite of all attempts to deny it, she experienced it with guilt and shame.

Today the misunderstandings about sexual guilt and repression in your world are almost as great as ever. The repressions and denials, the guilts and false shames are not merely a result of social mores and bigoted influences, but are actually products of the inability to carry the force of the fully unified power current, whose strength can be borne only by someone at least relatively liberated from negativity, fear, doubt, and destructiveness.

The strongly sexual person who experiences sexuality without love, without a deeply personal melding with a specifically chosen other, and who promiscuously chooses passing partners without heart and mind is essentially no different from the moralist who is faithful to a wife with whom he engages in surreptitious mating as a marital duty. Both are afraid of the love-sex current that is unified through the power of eros, through the power of mutuality in soul development, and commitment to each other through personal purification.

Toward Mystical Ecstasy

The man-woman relationship of the past and the attitude toward marriage are the direct results of the fear of the unified love-sex current. Self-purification was practically nonexistent for the average person, practiced only in the churches to any important degree. But there again, the full power of the current was diminished by the edict of celibacy. True, some specially gifted and advanced persons evoked this spiritual power through their own individual endeavors. *Mystical ecstasy is simply the release of a spiritual power current in which God is experienced as a living and physical reality.* This can also ideally happen through the melding of a man and a woman who are sufficiently free from fear, who follow together a path of self-purification. Their union will release the inner power current so that they will experience God in themselves and in each other.

Before discussing this experience further, let us go back to the evolutionary stages of history. The picture I painted about marriage is not very attractive. Marriage as it had existed for so long was truly a more sinful estate than all the sins which the moralists who perpetuated these standards condemned. These moralists directed the accusation of sin toward illicit sex, toward promiscuous or pornographic sex that could be outwardly identified. It is true that these acts do indicate denial of the God-given unification of love and sexuality, of the greatest power current, which is in itself an expression of the divine presence.

In a certain sense the fear and denial are symptoms of the unpurified soul—the fallen spirit, if you will. But since you all also fulfill a task in your return to the state of union with God, it is futile to rail against this. Those who do it are themselves fallen spirits, unpurified souls, and parts of the same evolutionary movement. The appropriate attitude toward fear of the full power current is acceptance; gentle training is needed so that the personality can gradually acclimatize itself to this high-powered force and bear it in comfort. Ecstasy can and will become comfortable as the soul grows in stature. This happens through a process of development over many incarnations.

The real sinfulness of the attitude toward marriage that prevailed until recently resulted from secondary guilt. Instead of admitting the fear of loving an equal, the man had to put down the woman. Instead of admitting fear of loving an equal and experiencing the pleasure of sexuality, the woman had to alienate herself from the man by making him the enemy. Instead of admitting that he feared an equal relationship, the man had to make the woman an object. Instead of admitting the fear of self-responsibility on all levels, the woman made herself an object and then blamed the man for this mutual creation. Both sexes denied the fear, which in a deeper sense might be called the primary guilt, a guilt that all people share.

The denial of the fear caused secondary guilts. Some of these secondary guilts gave power to lower-self energy. Material greed was fostered; money, power, and social advantage became motives for choosing mates. Mass images, appearances, idealized self-images were nourished; pride and vanity were elevated into false moral values. If you consider the moral indignation, the moral self-righteousness of men and women toward those who deviated from the accepted standards, you can see the strength of the secondary guilt. The mask-self claimed greed, calculating self-interest, prideful appearance values, and the mutual using of each other as the highest of moral standards. Such claims go way beyond ordinary hypocrisy. A hypocrisy so deep-rooted and so pernicious required a strong uprooting; otherwise the soul could not heal. It is important, my friends, for you to see the nature of the attitude toward marriage through many, many centuries. People marrying for love were the great exceptions.

The collective state of consciousness created these conditions in most marriages of the past. The same collective state of consciousness also created karmic conditions, prerequisites for specific guidance for subsequent incarnations. For example, the antagonism that generally existed between men and women had to manifest specifically between individual men and women to a much greater degree than it does now. It was often predestined that two such individuals had to meet as prospective marriage partners. Their elders would arrange it. This kind of union gave the scope to bring out in each person general and specific negative feelings and attitudes, which, once conscious, became the basis for transformation of those traits. Thus, my friends, the marriages made in heaven were by no means always positive unions of love and affection, attraction and respect. The negative mutuality between many individual men and women created the collective consciousness, created karmic conditions, and also created the standards of society.

A Great Leap in Collective Consciousness
In very recent times, consciousness made a great leap. Humanity has truly become ready to shed the old attitudes and create new conditions, new standards, new moral values. This can clearly be seen in your times by many drastic changes. The women's liberation movement, the sexual liberation movement,

and a very different attitude toward marriage are clearly signs of a newly emerging consciousness. These manifestations must be viewed in the light of an overall evolutionary direction, otherwise you cannot really grasp the inner meaning of the changes.

In all evolutionary movements the pendulum tends to swing from one extreme to another. This is at times inevitable, sometimes even desirable, provided the swings are limited. But when the swings are greater than necessary or desirable, fanaticism and blindness develop exactly as they did at the opposite extreme.

For example, today's sexual freedom is a reaction to the shackles of former times. To a degree this phase is necessary until the wisdom of the new consciousness becomes complete itself, and commitment to one mate is experienced as freer, more liberated, and infinitely more desirable than the uncommitted free-floating exchange of partners. The cycle had to move from involuntary monogamous commitment—with concomitant limitations on personal growth for both men and women—to recognition of the debilitating effects of this state of affairs and a consequent libertinism and polygamous expression. From there the movement can now proceed to a new groundedness in real inner freedom and independence that voluntarily chooses monogamous commitment because it yields infinitely more fulfillment.

A particularly pernicious aspect of the old attitude toward marriage was that the sexual need as well as the need for companionship were polluted by opportunistic, materialistic, and exploitative ends. Even worse, this pollution and displacement was looked upon as if it were morally desirable. *Whenever one soul current is put secretly into the service of another, both become negative.* If love, eros, and sex were given their rightful places, then the real needs for success, respect from the community, and material abundance could function in a higher-self way. Humanity had to break away from the distortion, and a certain amount of upheaval became inevitable. The sexual revolution had to manifest at times in undesirable ways—but undesirable only when seen out of context.

Of course, the true lessons must be learned individually. This lesson is exactly what I am talking about. The old ways desperately need profound change. *A new sexual expression and a joyful acceptance of the sexual drive has to emerge.* At the same time, individual men and women need to understand the enormous importance of the wholeness of love, eros, and sex; of affection and respect; of tenderness and passion; of trust and mutual partnership; of sharing and of helping one another. It must be therefore understood that advocating the committed relationship is not a moralizing edict whose purpose is to deprive you of pleasure. Quite the contrary is true. The power current evoked through a fusion between love, respect, passion, and sexuality is infinitely more ecstatic than any casual fusion could ever be. It is so powerful, in fact, that the very authorities against whom there has been so much rebellion have feared this combined current more than anyone. These authorities are not that far removed from those who allow themselves to experience sexuality only in a split-off way, cut off from the heart, ignorant of real intimacy and sharing.

The Ultimate Goal

Knowing the state into which you can and must eventually grow, because it is your innate destiny, is important. Without such a chart you cannot steer your ship. But there is a subtle yet distinct difference between organically following this model and attempting forcefully to be what you have not yet become. Accept that you cannot immediately be the ideal, totally fused individual. *You know that it takes a long time, much experience, many lessons, trials and errors, untold incarnations, until your soul emerges as a complete being. You need to know now that such a state exists, even if you are still quite unable to experience it.* You need to know it without self-pressure, without self-moralizing, without discouragement. All these forcing attitudes are destructive and erroneous.

The attempt to enforce an ideal standard that individuals

cannot possibly live up to has unfortunately been made by almost all organized religions. This is why organized religion has fallen into ill repute today. The state of wholeness should be placed lightly into your consciousness. It should never become a whip. It should merely be a reminder of who you essentially are already and who you already are in your essence and who you will one day fully become.

Just as it is foolish to turn into an atheist because of the errors of religion, so it is foolish to discard marriage altogether because of previous distortions. Before marriage began to be doubted as a valid institution by many, the attitude toward it had already begun to change considerably, especially in the last several decades. Individuals began to choose partners freely, motivated generally by love. This also often led to errors. Individuals who were too young and immature to form a really meaningful union chose marriage based on superficial attraction, without deep knowledge of self or partner. No wonder such marriages could not survive. But this step was necessary before maturity could be gained.

Just as individuals cannot learn unless they make mistakes, neither can the collective consciousness. New ways have to be tried by both before the soul can reach wisdom and truth. The freedom to choose independently, to experience sexual and erotic pleasure, to make mistakes and learn from them, to form different and more mature relationships as part of the growing process, without condemning less mature ones, are all necessary to learn the real significance of marriage. It has to be seen not as a shackle imposed by a moralizing outer or inner authority, but as a freely chosen gift, the greatest, most desirable state imaginable, the keenest pleasure and fulfillment for which the soul and the personality have to become strong, resilient, mature, and capable. *Bliss, ecstasy, pleasure supreme can never exist gratuitously, can never be cheaply snatched. They could not be borne that way. They can be borne only when the personality has reached sufficient purification, security, faith, self-knowledge, comprehension of the universe—Christness.*

Sexual liberation has to go through some stages that may seem exaggerated, or may even be exaggerated, before further sexual liberation—the unification of love, eros, and sex—can create the new marriage. Fleeting sexual encounters should not be looked upon as the final state of liberation. They are, at best, a very temporary and limited phase. No one who has ever experienced this stage has ever truly been satisfied by it, not even on the merely physical level. You may delude yourself into thinking that this is the best you could hope to experience, but it is not. You may deny your deeper unfulfilled longing because some of the hitherto unfulfilled longing has been assuaged. But you have so much further to go to give yourself what you really need, want, desire, and what you should indeed have.

As with the sexual revolution, women's liberation, too, had to go to some kind of extreme—at least temporarily. So some women had to become as hard, as unyielding as their greatest enemy, man, in order to experience their strength, their capacity to be independent, self-responsible, creative, and resourceful. As long as this is a passing phase from which further changes will emerge it is all right. But when this is seen as the final ideal, it becomes as damaging as being the suppressed and dependent child-woman you no longer want or need to be. The new woman combines independence, self-responsibility, full-fledged adulthood with the softness and yieldingness that was previously associated exclusively with the dependent parasite. The new man combines his heart feelings, his softness, his gentleness with his strength and abilities, not like the woman, but in a complementary way. The two can form the new marriage.

The New Marriage of Fusion and Transparency

The new marriage will not be formed early in life. If the participants are young, they will have reached considerable maturity as a result of a genuine, intense inner work, such as this path. The new marriage is a nucleus of strength, with the partners fortifying each other as well as others in a commonly undertaken task for the greater cause. The new marriage is totally open and transparent. There are no secrets whatever. The soul-processes of the partners are totally shared. This kind of openness and transparency has to be learned. It is a path within the path, as it were. Expose your difficulty in achieving this openness, rather than trying to deny or hide it. Part of the openness consists of revealing your fear of the strong spiritual current, of the forces released by the unification of your sexuality and your heart. When the fear is shared—even though you may be unable to shed it as yet—the obstructions will be eliminated relatively fast, and a kind of vibrant fulfillment will come from the sharing itself.

In the new marriage, being on a path of profound self-development and bringing into the light the hidden parts of the self are prerequisites to fulfillment in an alive and vibrant relationship. When the vibrancy ebbs away, the causes need to be explored by both partners together. There may be any number of reasons for the stagnation, none of them necessarily bad or shameful.

When all levels of the two personalities are open to each other, join, and finally fuse, the intensity and vibrancy of the sexual encounter will surpass anything you can at present imagine. You deeply long for it, because this fulfillment is your birthright and your destiny. It can exist only in a partnership such as I have described. This kind of fusion cannot come about easily. It is the result of infinite patience, growth, change, transformation. But it should live in your vision as a possibility you can indeed actualize one day.

The fusion on all levels of the personality means the fusion of all energy bodies. This is very rarely the case. You will come to know when the fusion exists only on the physical level, and when it happens on the emotional, mental, and spiritual levels. All these energy bodies exist in reality and can fuse or not according to prevailing conditions. *When the fusion takes place on all the levels, you not only become one with your partner, but with God.* You realize God in the mate and God in yourself. No wonder the power current is too strong to bear unless your personalities have reached a high degree of inner development and purification.

Once you realize that sexual fusion is insufficient and uninteresting unless it includes all the energy bodies in the process of coming together, your approach to a sexual encounter will become very different. Sexual union will never be casual or haphazard; *you will consider it a holy ritual.* These rituals will be created by the individual couples and may change over time. They will never deteriorate into fixed routines. The sexual encounter is a true fusion of the masculine and feminine principles as universal forces. Each sexual fusion will be a creative act, bringing forth new spiritual forms, new heights of development in the two selves that can be passed on to others. The complementary merging of these two divine aspects—the feminine and masculine forces—will create not only total fulfillment, ecstasy, and bliss, but enduring new values and a true experience of divine reality, of the Christ in the self and in the other.

My beloved friends, this lecture should encourage you, no matter how far away you may seem to be from fulfilling the destiny I outline here. You are moving in the right direction merely by being able to comprehend it. Choose to use it in the most positive way, no matter where you are. Knowing this truth will free you as any truth must, even if you cannot attain its realization yet. Rejoice that complete fusion exists, and that it waits for you.

With this, I bless you, my beloved ones. The Christ within your deepest soul fuses with the Christ consciousness and those energies that surround you and fill you with love, strength, and blessings.

Textual Note

Each chapter in this book is an edited version of a Guide lecture or lectures. Some have been shortened only slightly; some substantially. Since chapter titles are not always the same as the original titles of the lectures, we give here a listing of chapter numbers and the equivalent lecture numbers and titles.

Chapter 1, Relationship, is the second part of lecture #106, *"Sadness Versus Depression— Relationship,"* with one paragraph from lecture # 149, *"Cosmic Pull Toward Evolution."*

Chapter 2, The Masculine and Feminine Principles in the Creative Process, is lecture #169.

Chapter 3, The Forces of Love, Eros, and Sexuality is lecture #44. This lecture appeared also in *The Pathwork of Self-Transformation*, Bantam 1990.

Chapter 4, The Spiritual Significance of Relationship, is lecture #180. This lecture appeared also in *The Pathwork of Self-Transformation.*

Chapter 5, Mutuality: A Cosmic Principle and Law, is lecture #185.

Chapter 6, Desire for Unhappiness and Fear of Loving, is a combination of lectures #58, *"Desire for Happiness and Desire for Unhappiness,"* and #72, *"Fear of Loving."*

Chapter 7, The Valid Desire to Be Loved, is the second part of lecture #69, with an answer to a question from lecture #75, *"Questions and Answers."*

Chapter 8, Objectivity and Subjectivity in Relationship, is the second part of lecture #42.

Chapter 9, Compulsion to Re-create and Overcome Childhood Hurts, is lecture #73. This lecture appeared also in *The Pathwork of Self-Transformation* and in *Fear No Evil,* Pathwork Press 1993.

Chapter 10, Attachment of the Life Force to Negative Situations, is the second part of #135, *"Mobility in Relaxation— Attachment of the Life Force to Negative Situations"* plus a section from lecture #49, *"Guilt: Justified and Unjustified— Obstacles on the Path."* This part of lecture #135 also appears in *Fear No Evil.*

Chapter 11, Life, Love, and Death, is lecture #123, *"Overcoming Fear of the Unknown."*

Chapter 12, From Unconscious Negative Interaction to Conscious Choice of Love is lecture #202, *"Psychic Interaction of Negativity,"* plus one Question and Answer from lecture #133, *"Love as Spontaneous Soul Movement."*

Chapter 13, The Spiritual Significance of Sexuality, is lecture #207.

Chapter 14, The New Woman and the New Man, is lecture #229, *"Woman and Man in the New Age."*

Chapter 15, The New Marriage, is lecture #251, *"New Age Marriage."*

List of Pathwork Lectures

1. The Sea of Life
2. Decisions and Tests
3. Choosing Your Destiny
4. World Weariness
5. Happiness as a Link in the Chain of Life
6. Man's Place in the Spiritual and Material Universes
7. Asking for Help and Helping Others
8. Contact with God's Spirit World – Mediumship
9. The Lord's Prayer
10. Male and Female Incarnations – Their Rhythm and Causes
11. Know Thyself
12. The Order and Diversity of the Spiritual Worlds –
    The Process of Reincarnation
13. Positive Thinking
14. The Higher Self, the Lower Self, and the Mask
15. Influence between the Spiritual and Material Worlds
16. Spiritual Nourishment
17. The Call
18. Free Will
19. Jesus Christ
20. God – the Creation
21. The Fall
22. Salvation
25. The Path
26. Finding One's Faults
27. Escape Possible Also on the Path
28. Communication with God
29. Activity and Passivity
30. Self-Will, Pride, and Fear
31. Shame
32. Decision-Making
33. Occupation with Self
34. Preparation for Reincarnation
35. Turning to God
36. Prayer
37. Acceptance – Dignity in Humility
38. Images
39. Image-Finding
40. More on Images
41. Images – the Damage They Do
42. Objectivity and Subjectivity
43. Three Basic Personality Types: Reason, Will, Emotion

These lectures are available from the centers listed on the following page.

For further information about the Pathwork:

A number of active Pathwork Centers and a network of many groups study and work with the Pathwork lectures in North and South America, and in Europe. We welcome the opportunity to support you in connecting with others who are interested in exploring this material further. To order any Pathwork lecture or books, or for further information, please contact the following regional centers marked with an asterisk (*):

California & Southwest:
Pathwork of California, Inc.*
1355 Stratford Court #16
Del Mar, California 92014
(619) 793-1246 Fax (619) 259-5224

Great Lakes Region:
Great Lakes Pathwork*
1117 Fernwood
Royal Oak, Michigan 48067
(313) 585-3984

Mid-Atlantic and South:
Sevenoaks Pathwork Center*
Route 1, Box 86
Madison, Virginia 22727
(703) 948-6544 Fax (703) 948-5508

New York, New Jersey, New England:
Phoenicia Pathwork Center*
Box 66
Phoenicia, New York 12464
(914) 688-2211 Fax (914) 688-2007

Northwest:
The Northwest Pathwork*
c/o Kathleen Goldberg
811 NW 20th, Suite 103C
Portland, Oregon 97209
(503) 223-0018

Philadelphia:
Philadelphia Pathwork*
c/o Carolyn Tilove
910 S. Bellevue Avenue
Hulmeville, Pennsylvania 19407
(215) 752-9894

Brazil:
Aidda Pustilnik*
Rua da Graviola #264, Apt. 1003
41810-420 Itaigara Salvador, Brasil
Ph. 71-2470068 Fax 71-245-3089

Canada:
Ottawa/Montreal Pathwork
Roddy Duchesne
604-222 Guigues Ave.
Ottawa, Ontario K1N 5J2 Canada
Ph. (613) 241-4982

Germany:
Pfadgruppe Kiel
Paul Czempin
Lüdemannstrasse 51
24114 Kiel Germany
Ph. 0431-66-58-07

Holland:
Padwerk*
Johan Kos
Boerhaavelaan 9
1401 VR Bussum, Holland
Ph/Fax 02159-35222

Italy:
Il Sentiero*
Raffaele Iandolo
Campodivivo, 43. 04020 Spigno
Saturnia (LT) Italy
Ph. (39) 771-64463

Mexico:
Andres Leites*
Tulipanes 148, Col. del Bosque
Cuernavaca, Mor 62150 Mexico
Ph. 73-132144 Fax 73-113592

Foreign translations of Pathwork materials are available in Dutch, French, German, Italian, Portuguese and Spanish.